EATEN BY THE JAPANESE

This shocking and poignant story of World War II and its forgotten Indian Prisoners of War has never been told before from the viewpoint of an ordinary Indian soldier who was right in the middle of the action. Nor has such a story ever been coupled with a moving story of fathers and sons. Fifty-one years after it was written, John Baptist Crasta's book was published by his son, Richard Crasta, and has received praise from a variety of critics and readers, including the Chief of Staff of the Indian Army at the time of its launch, General V. P. Malik.

"More than any book in recent memory, *Eaten by the Japanese* drives home the lasting effects of enforced captivity – not only on the bodies but also on the minds of the prisoners. It is a book about kindness, solidarity, and collective survival, about the bonds that matter: those between one single human being and another. Not for the sake of vengeance, for there is none of that spirit in this book, but for the sake of memory, the memory of the epic struggle that changed our world and opened it to liberation, these agonies must be remembered by our generation."
    —Barry Fruchter, Ph.D., Professor
    Nassau Community College, New York

"A tale of unmitigated horror. A handsome tribute to a man of courage and rectitude."
–Khushwant Singh, Author

"Together with the essays by Richard Crasta, this well-printed memoir . . . is a moving tribute to the Unknown Indian Soldier."—*The Deccan Herald*

John Baptist Crasta

EATEN BY THE JAPANESE

THE MEMOIR OF AN UNKNOWN INDIAN PRISONER OF WAR

JOHN BAPTIST CRASTA

EDITED WITH ESSAYS AND A BIOGRAPHICAL INTRODUCTION

BY

RICHARD CRASTA

First published in India in 1998 in a limited edition by Invisible Man Books, this book was then published in a fully revised and annotated edition with new epilogues by Invisible Man Press, Inc, New York in 1999.

This 2012 paperback edition is published by The Invisible Man Press, New York, and includes a new essay by Richard Crasta in addition to the original three essays, and additional biographical material. Richard Crasta is also the son of the late John Baptist Crasta (who died in 1999), and the author of 12 other books.

For more information on this and forthcoming Invisible Man Books, please visit http://www.richardcrasta.com

Disclaimer and Co-Author's Request

This book was published by Richard Crasta (editor and minor co-author) on the basis of an untitled handwritten manuscript of John Baptist Crasta. All other subjective interpretations, footnotes, and essays that follow the main memoir are those of the son, who requests that his father and this book be judged solely on the basis of the actual memoir.

Important: Please note that the *Footnotes* and the *Notes* (two separate chapters) contain some very significant additional clarifying information that may help place a few of the events in context.

DEDICATION

For my mother, Nathalia

CONTENTS

Comparative Table of Ranks

(starting from the lowest upwards)

BRITISH	INDIAN	AMERICAN
Private	Sepoy	Private
Lance Corporal	Lance Naik	Lance Corporal
Corporal	Naik	Corporal
Sergeant	Havildar	Sergeant
Company Quarter Master-Sergeant (CQMS)	Company Quarter Master-Havildar (CQMH)	
Company Sergeant-Major (CSM)	Company Havildar-Major (CHM)	
Regimental Sergeant-Major (RSM) (A warrant-officer, assisting the Adjutant of a Regiment or Battalion)	Regimental Havildar-Major (RHM)	Regimental Sergeant-Major (RSM) (The highest-ranking Non-Commissioned Officer)

Viceroy's Commissioned Officers (World War II) (VCOs) and Junior Commissioned Officers (JCOs) (Present Indian Army)

BRITISH	INDIAN	AMERICAN
Regimental Sergeant-Major (warrant-officer)	Jemadar (WWII) or Naib Subedar (present) Subedar Subedar-Major (SM)	Sergeant-Major

Note: VCOs/JCOs are also OR (Other Ranks), the definition of "Other Ranks" being "soldiers *other* than commissioned officers." ICOs are Indian Commissioned Officers.

John Baptist Crasta

ACKNOWLEDGMENTS (1999, 2012)

The author, and his son and publisher/editor, wish to acknowledge the help of the Japanese and others who helped the author during the War, including those who restrained themselves from eating the author, thus making this narrative possible.

They also wish to acknowledge the following: the generous and splendidly gracious Col. Cyrus Dalal, as well as Sunney Tharappan, Barry Fruchter, Brigadier Ferris, and David and Faye Cohen of Florida for having encouraged him with the project and provided a sympathetic and critical audience for his essays. Richard Crasta also wishes to thank General V.P. Malik, former Chief of Staff of the Indian Army, for his kind words and the audience given to him, and Dhirendra Singh, former Home Secretary of India, for his encouragement and support.

Finally, they would like to acknowledge the love and support of Christine, wife of John Baptist Crasta, and mother of Richard Crasta, and of all others who helped make this book possible.

Eaten by the Japanese

The Memoir of an Unknown Indian Prisoner of War

John Baptist Crasta

John Baptist Crasta

IN SINGAPORE, LIFE WAS GAY

When Britain, fighting the Second World War, began to mobilize its Indian resources of whatever kind — vegetable, mineral, or animal — my unit, 12 FB, was mobilized at Ambala[1] early in 1941. In early March 1941, orders were received to proceed overseas. Although the destination was a secret, on the day of the move, 13 March 1941, I came to know that it would be Singapore. At that time, any man who got a posting to Singapore was considered the luckiest; and naturally, I was overjoyed. We left by a special troop-carrying train and arrived in Bombay on 16 March 1941. On the same day, we embarked on the H.T. Neurihor — a fine trooper of maybe twelve to fourteen thousand tons. With us were several other units of draftees, making a total of roughly 15,000 men. In the same convoy was another transport carrying the 9th Indian Division.

I was allotted a second class cabin. The accommodation, food, and recreational arrangements were excellent. After a few hours of zigzag sailing, our convoy headed southwards, thus confirming my previous information regarding our destination. Along with me was a fellow-passenger who had lived in Singapore before. He started his cock and bull stories about the fascinations of Malaya and the amusements in store for us. As

---

[1] A major army cantonment in Northern India.

we sailed, we could see in the Indian Ocean huge fish —
dolphins and other forms of sea life — cutting somersaults in
the blue waters, diving and coming up again. Sometimes, one of
these monsters would race over the surface of the water, and
others would follow. We also saw huge whales, as big as
mountains, moving easily. It was a grand sight.

We reached Singapore on 26 March 1941 and disembarked.
We were taken to No.7, M.R.C., Bidadure, about 8 miles from
the harbor.

Our first impression of Singapore was that of a dreamland
— picturesque scenery, beautiful tiled buildings against a green
background, wide cemented roads, trams, buses, and cars.

Arrangements in the M.R.C. were not satisfactory. We were
provided with tents to be pitched on uneven ground covered
with grass. We had to level the ground ourselves. Also, the full
scale of rations was not issued. For instance meat, which is
authorized for service personnel in the field, was not issued for
several days until after our arrival. The reason was that the
camp staff was quite irresponsible and was only trying to make
a fortune. The camp Subedar Major, Head Clerk, Quarter
Master Jemadar, and Jemadar Adjutant were all in cahoots.

A month passed and no orders of posting were received. On
approaching our Administrative Headquarters (HQ 125PC), we
were told to wait for a few days more. Orders were
subsequently received for the despatch of a subsection (roughly
13 men) to Kuala Krai. The rest of 12 FB was moved to Buller
Camp, a place seven to eight miles away.

Buller Camp was on the tip of a small hill — a quiet place
amidst trees. We were attached to 35 LMC for discipline and
were given rental accommodation near this unit. Our bakers
were to work in the RASC (Royal Army Service Corps) Bakery
at Alexandria a mile away.

This bakery was machine-fitted and electrically run. It
turned out thirty to forty thousand loaves daily, kneading and
baking automatically. The loaves turned out were not as tasty
and fine as those hand-kneaded and baked in field ovens. Our
bakers worked two shifts — one day and one night.

I had little work to do. I was in the lines for the whole day, and when the Jemadar was ill or out, I was supervising the men in the bakery. This idle life did not please me as I wanted a responsible job in a big office. I applied for a transfer to the 2nd Echelon HQ 125 PS. However, they did not agree, and transferred me to 202 SPS on 10 September 1941.

Life in Singapore was very gay. Money was easily earned and spent. A Singapore dollar (worth one rupee eight annas in Indian currency) was worth nothing. The nightlife of Singapore presented several attractions. One could see Chinese rickshawwallahs moving to and fro with their passengers, and neatly dressed men and women making towards cabarets and cinema houses. Crowds waiting in front of soda water fountains in Chinese shops decorated with colored lights, and men having tea in hotels — all were out to spend a carefree evening after the day's work. Particular mention may be made of amusement halls named New World, Happy World, Great World etc., to which huge crowds started flocking after 8 PM. The entrance ticket was 10 cents. Within the enclosure, however, one found beer shops served by Chinese girls, cinema shows, drama, ballet, dancing, and the Malayan dance pageantry.

It was a peaceful crowd. The Chinese who formed the majority were a peace-loving people, as were the Malays. Malay music is sweet. Houses of ill fame and prostitution were rampant in Singapore. In a locality called Jallai Bassa, Chinese pros[2] would line up looking as attractive as possible with rouge, lipstick, and face powder, waiting for clients to choose them. After having been chosen, the girl would lead the man to her apartment.

Things were not too dear, although money was spent as easily as earned.

Life for the troops in Malaya left nothing to be desired. Electrified huts were provided for accommodation. There was plenty of water and good scenery. Food was ample and

---

[2] My father's coy word for prostitutes.

wholesome. Beer and liquor were made available in moderate quantities in canteens, and other amusements such as camp cinemas and picnics were arranged. Discipline was not too exacting.

Even in the topmost circles, war was not expected in Malaya, especially after the commencement of the German-Russian hostilities. Would Japan be so foolhardy as to wage a war against the might of Britain (India automatically included) and her allies the Australians and perhaps the Americans, when she was already engaged in a war with China? It was improbable and so the civilians and the military continued in their revelry. In the middle of 1941 Japanese troops and navy began their southward advance, occupying Saigon and other strategic positions in Indo-China. The French authorities, for obvious reasons, were compelled to yield.

In SPT, I had a very busy time. The section comprised roughly of sixty men. In addition, a POL (Petrol, Oil and Lubricants) section, Bakery section, and a Labor Detail had to be administered. Captain NNK was the senior officer with Lt. L.G.B. Fleming and Lt. Allen, who were later relieved by Lt. D. McCarthy as assistants. As Head Clerk, I had to reorganize the whole office, which was in a complete mess due to a lack of trained clerks. I was, therefore, forced to work nearly sixteen hours a day. The function of our section was to supply rations to the whole of 11 Division and certain non-Division units in addition to performing the duties of Station Transport Officer. The Depot was situated in the thick of rubber trees, a mile or two from Division HQ. Our staff was overworked.

The enemy was making feverish preparations for the attack, whereas our indifference to the imminent danger did not diminish. The gay life of the civilians and the military continued.

A notable event was a state visit from one of the high dignitaries of the neighboring State, Thailand, to Malaya. This gentleman, as the representative of a friendly independent power, was given a royal welcome and taken round the defences of Singapore. He expressed great satisfaction at what he saw. Thailand reiterated its determination to maintain absolute neutrality and to resist to the utmost any power who might encroach on her territory. This assurance gave great satisfaction to the British General Staff, who counted on Thailand's neutrality and resistance even in the "doubtful probability" of the Japanese invading Malaya through Thailand.

.

John Baptist Crasta

THE JAPANESE INVASION BEGINS

At the end of November 1941, it appeared that war was imminent. "Degree of Readiness" orders were issued. The Japanese started pouring into Thailand with the active cooperation of the Thai Government. The Military Command ordered the moving of certain units into Thailand. These units penetrated nearly twenty-five miles, and clashes started on 7 December 1941. Another invasion party tried landing in a sea craft at Kota Baharu. On the 8th morning at about 7 AM, a huge explosion was heard near our Depot; and on seeing the staff's concern, our Officer-in-charge (Captain W.J.P.) was heard saying that our RAF was practicing; whereas, what had actually happened was that the SRT aerodrome was being hammered by the Japanese bombers! The telephones started ringing. Only then was it officially announced that war had been declared.

No words can describe the confusion that prevailed. I was ordered to move to Bukit Mertajam, where Captain NNK had already gone to start an Advance Base Supply Depot. The days that followed were of high nervous tension. We saw lorries and motorcycles moving at top speed, conveying defeated men, both Indian and British, retreating. They had apparently abandoned their armies. Groups of soldiers were retreating on foot, their faces aghast with fear, their clothes and boots tattered and torn. They appeared badly shaken. They had only a few words to say, words like: *Oh, the Japanese are terrible. We are gone. There is no hope.*

Each day that passed saw more and more troops running backwards. We in Bukit Mertajam stood calm. Thousands of tons of stores were being received by rail from Singapore and had to be cleared and stored. Penang, about twenty miles from Bukit Mertajam, could be heard being mercilessly pounded by Japanese bombers. We had no air force to give them combat. The Japanese were determined to take Penang at any cost and so bombarded it mercilessly, killing thousands of civilians. The military, hardly a brigade, retreated to the mainland without loss, leaving the civilians to their fate. By 13 December 1941 Penang was taken, and on the morning of 16 December 1941, the enemy arrived at SPT. Our troops, after giving a hard battle at Alor Setar, retreated. In this the Leicester and Gurkha Battalions gave a good fight but were nearly wiped out. The same morning, Col. A.E.S., our Administrative Head, came to our depot and ordered us to retreat after destroying all supplies. A detail of Sappers & Miners was ordered to burn down a dump of 600,000 gallons of petrol and we got ready to move by 9 AM. Just then, the Commanding Officer, RIASC (Royal Indian Army Service Corps) 19th Division, Lt. Col. G.M. Lytton, came there and wanted three days' rations for the whole Division. He was not aware of the OC RASC's (Officer Commanding Royal Army Services Corps') order to move. This showed that there was no liaison between the two. Each of the services was trying to override the other.

We started at about 10 AM (Capt. NNK and myself in a car, last of all) and arrived in Ipoh the same afternoon to find the town being heavily bombarded by the Japanese. We stayed with the personnel of 205 SPS (Captains D.J. Mellon and P.W. Howell) for two days. Great confusion prevailed owing to frequent enemy raids whereas our own air force was never seen giving battle.

After the enemy planes had completely vanished, we could, however, see a couple of Brewster Buffaloes[3] cutting somersaults in the air, only to disappear again in the event of any sign of approaching Japanese planes. The personnel of 205 SPS and troops who had come to draw supplies would, when the air raid signal sounded, run helter skelter: some into the trenches and some into the jungles as far as their feet could carry them. At later stages, the Air Raid Precaution system completely broke down. The volunteers, apparently having tired of the whole business, threw away their whistles and looked for shelter themselves.

On 19 December 1941, we left for Kuala Kubu Baharu where we opened a Ration Dump with the cooperation of the District Officer, Perak. The troops holding positions in the vicinity were being catered for by us. One of the most decisive battles was being fought on the banks of the Perak River. For a week, nothing untoward happened.

---

[3] Originally an American Navy fighter, also used by the Royal Air Force during World War II.

John Baptist Crasta

THE QUICK MARCH TO SURRENDER

At the end of December 1941, more troops could be seen retreating south every day, some from the eastern coast where they had been holding an aerodrome. Our own ration strength was gradually being reduced daily, with the result that by the 5th or 6th January 1942, nobody came to draw rations. Where had they gone and what was the matter? If everybody had retreated, were we the only men to be left; and why didn't we receive orders for our move as well? These thoughts struck me and I mentioned these to my officer, Capt. NNK. He, however, seemed least perturbed and replied that if the situation was really dangerous, we would be ordered to evacuate. In any case, unless we heard from the O.C., Royal Army Service Corps, Kuala Lumpur, he said, we would have to stay there even if it meant falling into enemy hands! Incidentally, telephone connections had also broken down. How could we get in touch with Kuala Lumpur, or they with us? On the 7 January 1942, I became restless and again prevailed upon my Commanding Officer that something must be done, and that, too, immediately. He, therefore, agreed to send me and a Viceroy's Commissioned Officer to Kuala Lumpur to get orders from the OC RASC. The OC was very glad to see us and said that the situation was very dangerous, the enemy was only four miles from our dump and that we must "run" immediately. He was sorry he could not send us a message owing to breakdown of communications, but he blamed the Commander, RIASC 11 Division, who according to him ought to have issued us movement orders.

The Viceroy's Commissioned Officer returned to Kuala Kubu Baharu with these instructions, but now there was no time to burn the rations. The civil authorities had evacuated the station a week earlier. So, a portion of the rations were distributed to the Chinese civilians and the rest handed over to the Kuber of the Sikh Gurdwara with instructions to hand over the rations to the military in case anyone called.

The section then moved to Kuala Lumpur. A complaint was lodged that because of the failure of the administrative authorities to instruct us to evacuate, we had nearly fallen into enemy hands.

On 10 January 1942, we moved south to open another supply dump. The town was being heavily bombarded by the enemy. More soldiers, motorbikes, and soldier-laden jeeps were moving south at top speed. We left Tampin on 16 January to open a Supply Dump at Rengam (eighty miles south) in Johore State. We camped there until 24 January and arrived in Singapore on 25 January 1942. Our convoy was apparently noticed by the enemy. Hardly had we traveled twenty miles when half a dozen bombers appeared as if from the clouds, dived low, and dropped a couple of bombs. One fell just a few yards in front of our first lorry. The driver panicked and fled the vehicle without applying the brakes; as a result, the lorry capsized. Fortunately only two of our men received minor injuries.

On 27 January 1942, I was ordered to report to the DDST (Deputy Director Supply & Transport, Movement Control) Office for duty. The DDST was an Imperial formation with about 25 British clerks including lady typists. Indian clerks were attached to it for RIASC personnel work only. The office was located in HQ M.C. Fort Canning.

By 1 February our troops, having blown up the causeway spanning Singapore to the Mainland, retreated to Singapore Island which was then declared to be under siege.

The next few days saw heavy shelling and bombardment of the Singapore fortress. The bombers would swoop down, hit targets as they wished, and fly back into the sky. Our antiaircraft unit did not fire for fear of disclosure of position.

Were we so helpless that the enemy raiders could come and go according to their will and pleasure as if they were the sole masters of the island? Could this be called a war?

The situation was very tense during the first week of February 1942. The fate of Singapore, the "invincible" fortress with its floating docks worth eight million pounds, was hanging in the balance. The enemy had taken up positions in Johore and might effect a landing in Singapore any day. Fighting was confined to exchange of artillery fire on the morning of 8 February 1942 at 1 AM. Under cover of heavy artillery barrage, the Japanese succeeded in landing in rubber boats. Casualties in their ranks were heavy; but as they were superior in number, this did not matter to them. At the same time, more landings were effected on the West coast of the fortress by soldiers traveling part of the distance by rubber boats and then by swimming. Heavy bombing and shelling followed, making confusion worse confounded. The Japanese succeeded in capturing aerodromes in Tengah and Changi.

On the nights of 10 February and 11 February 1942, I could hear the sound of machine guns, tommy guns, and hand grenades only two or three miles from Alexandria, and our heavy, fifteen-inch guns located there were firing incessantly causing a deafening roar and shaking our barracks to their very foundations; this noise affected my ears for a long time, causing severe ache.

On 12 February 1942, all the 12 SPC personnel (about 1100 men) left Buller Camp to take shelter in a huge civil building in the heart of the city. I, too, went with them, although the chief clerk of Deputy Directorate Supply & Transport had no objection to our moving there. Several bombs fell near our building but apart from splinters breaking windowpanes, no casualties occurred among us. The C-in-C of the Japanese forces (Lt. Gen. Yamashita) demanded an unconditional surrender, failing which he threatened the stoppage of water supply and the complete annihilation of the city. Leaflets were dropped advising the civilians and Indian troops to take cover.

With a view to dispersing units in the event of a concentrated air raid, my section (202 SPS) and certain others were ordered to move to 55 Godown. The senior officer there told us that he could not accommodate us; whereupon, we were taken to Ferrers Park. This place was under heavy shelling. We could see barracks burning and sentries dying. We did not know what to do. There was a small covered trench sufficient to accommodate hardly ten men. Forty of us squeezed ourselves into it. Shells began falling all around. We nearly got suffocated inside; and, added to this, the blast and fumes from burst shells entered the trench. Our men — all boys not more than twenty-one years old — were very scared. To remain inside a little longer would mean certain death. I thought it better to die outside than to be choked inside. So I came out. At a distance, I could hear an Australian driver asking our Captain whether he would like to escape, leaving the Indians there. This, I thought, was too much. I at once went to the Captain and told him that all of us would like to run away from there. He reluctantly agreed and looked for the lorry which had brought us there. The Malay driver had taken to his heels leaving the vehicle there. Our Officer Commanding then prevailed upon the Australian driver to give us his lorry. He agreed and drove us back to the building from which we had come. That was the night of 14 February 1942. The 15th saw another day of the heaviest bombardment and shelling. The enemy, having pushed forward, was converging on the heart of the city. The General Headquarters was under siege. In the afternoon, our force commander deputed a staff officer with a white flag to surrender. The staff officer was taken by the Japanese to General Yamashita, who wanted the British General and the Governor themselves to negotiate with him.

16

Unconditional surrender was signed at about 4 PM in the Ford Factory at Bukit Timah, and the cease fire order was given. But owing to the dispersal of troops, firing did not cease until 7 PM.

We were informed of the surrender at 8 PM. This news came as a great relief to everyone.

We heard that some British officers and Other Ranks[4] had preferred to shoot themselves rather than fall into the hands of the Japanese. A rumour had it that the enemy would not accept British currency. Many of the British officers and soldiers, mostly Gurkhas, burnt whatever currency notes they had.

---

[4] Viceroy's Commissioned Officers and Junior Commissioned Officers are also considered to be Other Ranks, the definition of "Other Ranks" being "soldiers *other* than commissioned officers." .

John Baptist Crasta

SURRENDER AND SEDUCTION

On the morning of 16 February 1942, orders were issued that all Indian prisoners should gather at Ferrers Park and the British at Changi at 9 AM on the following day. We could now see the Japanese soldiers driving triumphantly into the city to the reluctant cheers of the civilians.

The next day, we marched to Ferrers Park, where over 60,000 prisoners had collected for the surrender ceremony. Lt. Col. W.R. Hunt informed us that we were their prisoners and were being handed over to the Japanese, and were to be subject to their discipline. Then, on behalf of the British General Staff, he handed us to Major Fujiwara, officer of the Japanese General Staff; and having signed the surrender papers, left. Major Fujiwara spoke to us in Japanese (his speech translated into English by Lt. Kunizuku) at length as to how the mighty British forces in Malaya and the invincible fortress of Singapore had been destroyed in such a short time. He added that they were fighting the common Anglo-Saxon enemy of the Asiatics, and that theirs was a noble cause. The Whites, who mercilessly exploited the Asiatics, must be driven out of the entire continent. This sacred war championed by Nippon was not for selfish reasons, but for the sake of all Asians. The Emperor had commanded that all Indians be treated like their brothers, and he hoped that Indians would themselves try to throw off the yoke of slavery. He would now hand us over to the command of our officers, and had released Captain Mohan Singh for that purpose. We must carry out the latter's orders as if they came from the Japanese themselves.

Amidst thunderous applause "Captain" Mohan Singh mounted the rostrum and spoke for over two hours. He told us that British Imperialism had reduced India to a state of abject poverty, degradation, and humiliation in the eyes of the world. Even a much smaller nation like the Japanese had taken up cudgels and was out to crush the Anglo-Saxon might. They were succeeding because the spirit of unity and self-sacrifice was imbibed by them. The Japanese soldier led a very simple life; his pay was only a meager sum of four to seven rupees a month. His discipline and honesty were of the highest order.

Captain Singh mentioned an incident in which a Japanese soldier was caught stealing a watch from another. The culprit was brought before the Officer Commanding who made him stand in the sun, and slapped and kicked him violently. When the officer got tired, he would retire, rest awhile, come back, and again proceed with the slapping and kicking. This continued the whole day, but the soldier would not move or cry. He stood there like a post until his officer dismissed him late in the evening. This was only one example of the Japanese soldier's high sense of discipline, Captain Singh said.

He wanted Indian soldiers to emulate the Japanese. They were our Asiatic brothers, he said, and they had promised full support to drive out the British from India. Many Indians had helped the Japanese in the early stages of the war, but even without Indian help, the Japanese would have conquered Malaya, although their victory would have been delayed by a week. "We are going to start a national army which every Indian must join. And with the help of the Japanese, we are going to drive out the British," he said. Brotherly treatment would be meted out to those who joined. He would look after our comforts. This, however, did not mean complete exemption from manual labor!

20

He then asked the prisoners to raise their hands if they wished to join the INA.[5] All the men assembled there put up their hands (some even two at a time). Cries of "Inquilab Zindabad! Hindustan Azad!"[6] rent the air. The Japanese seem jubilant over this. No sooner was this over than I could see several faces becoming sad. One person (H.L.) started crying like a child, muttering, "I have served my masters for twenty-five years. What will I have to do now? What will become of my family? Oh God ...." This only goes to illustrate the peculiar situation: how the privations of a one-sided campaign, defections, despair, discouragement, and a sense of helplessness overcome a soldier when he is deprived of his arms. Some of the men were carried away by a strong although familiar anti-British feeling.

So the crowd dispersed with orders to collect at different Prisoners of War camps according to groups of units. We were assigned to Bidadare B camp, In-charge Lt. Col. J.U. Bhonsle. We had a total strength of 1,100 Royal Indian Army Service Corps personnel (senior officer being Capt. N.N.Khosk) and other fighting units. The Japanese demanded cent per cent[7] fatigue,[8] excluding only the sick and the kitchen staff. The fatigue hours lasted nearly twelve hours. Our men had to march over eight miles, clear debris caused by the bombing and shelling, also clear the streets, et cetera.

The ration consisted of warranty-expired *atta*[9] and rice preserved in lime, which caused dysentery among the prisoners and exacted a toll of over five thousand lives in a couple of

---

[5] The Indian National Army, an organization dedicated to freeing India from the British through armed means. It was started by Subhash Chandra Bose, a charismatic nationalist leader who disagreed with Gandhi's strategy of using only nonviolent means. Jailed by the British, he escaped to become the founder of the INA. He died in a plane crash in 1945, though rumours of his survival have continued for decades. See Notes for further commentary.

[6] "Long Live Freedom! Independence to India!"

[7] The Indian English term for 100 percent.

[8] Compulsory labour.

[9] Wheat Flour.

months. Medical facilities were nonexistent. The Japanese seemed unconcerned, and it was a long time before Indian doctors organized medical relief.

On 1 March 1942 we were ordered to move to Kranji, near the Johore causeway. From there our men would go daily to Tengah to build an aerodrome, marching nearly ten miles to work. It was, therefore, thought more convenient to move the men to Tengah itself, so we moved to Tengah on 15 April 1942. The accommodation that we got there was not even fit for animals. Sleeping span of eight spaces[10] per man was allotted. The thatched roof of the barracks was torn and tattered, allowing insects and worms inside. There was hardly enough water to drink; and as the men were overworked, they had no time to bathe or wash clothes, which caused further stench. Until then not a single cent had been paid to us by the Japanese for our labor. On repeated representations being made, they agreed to pay ten cents per day only to those who actually did fatigue. This amount, roughly $3 (four rupees and eight annas) a month, was hardly sufficient to buy even soap.

The meetings of senior officers were being held almost daily in Bidadare, which was the Supreme HQ of the INA, but unanimity never existed. "Captain" Mohan Singh was the Supreme Commander (General Officer Commanding in Chief) of the INA forces with unlimited powers over the prisoners. He had, along with all the men of 1/14 Punjab Regiment, joined hands with the Japanese in the early stages of the war in Thailand and carried on incessant propaganda in Indian lines. He exhorted Indian soldiers not to fight the Japanese but to put down arms and join him. The Japanese were their brothers and would treat them well. It was no use fighting as the Japanese could never be defeated. If they resisted, they would be put to death. This propaganda, however, failed to have any effect on certain units.

At last, the four Bidadare resolutions were passed; and Officers Commanding various units were instructed to collect

---

[10] One Space equaled about 4 inches (about 10cm).

names of volunteers. It was apparent that many of the senior officers did not wish to collaborate actively with the Japanese in a war against the British; but in view of the delicate situation, they could not get out of it altogether. That would mean bringing on the wrath of the Japanese and endangering their lives. Caught between the devil and the deep sea, they tried to fashion a compromise which would satisfy the Japanese for the time being and at the same time not offend the British. The four Bidadare Resolutions were vaguely worded and suited their purpose. The senior officers presumably assured the Supreme Commander of the wholehearted cooperation of all the ranks under their respective charges.

A vigorous propaganda campaign was carried out for enrollment; but out of a total of sixty-five thousand prisoners, only about twenty-five thousand accepted. Non-volunteers were threatened with hard fatigue and being taken to distant places which might mean their end. The powers that be were aghast at the poor response. In what way could the "Supreme Commander" satisfy the Japanese, whom he had assured of the support of all the Indian troops? Somehow or the other, he must succeed.

Thus, "Captain" Mohan Singh got an idea. Near Bidadare, a camp was created to torture non-volunteers. Although given the innocent name of Separation Camp, it was actually a concentration camp where the most inhuman atrocities were committed by INA men on their non-volunteer Indian brethren. Subedars Sher Singh and Fateh Khan were put in charge of this notorious prison. High ranking officers who refused to have anything to do with the INA were thrown into it without clothing or food, made to carry heavy loads on their heads, and to double up on the slightest sign of slackness. They would be beaten by sweepers,[11] the infamous Nimboo having been put in charge of them. They would be caned, beaten, and

---

[11] A class of persons, very low in the Indian social or caste hierarchy, whose function was to sweep floors and latrines. To be beaten by a sweeper would be, to an Indian, adding insult to injury.

kicked. Various other devices of torture, perhaps copied from the Germans, were introduced. Many people died in that camp. Others were removed to a hospital only to die a slow death. Some others, not being able to bear the hardships, agreed to "sign" and were released. Sher Singh and Fateh Khan stood unmoved, still thirsting for blood.

Capt. NNK lectured to us at length that the four Bidadare resolutions meant nothing and that, if at all a chance occurred, we could still come out of it. And so he marched off with eight hundred RIASC men who agreed to the resolutions. Three hundred RIASC men, and a large number of other units, notably Mysore Infantry, Hyderabad Infantry, 2/10 Baluch, 9/19 Hyderabad were left at Tengah. We were running short of rations and a rumor was spread that we would be starved to death; however, we were much relieved to find supplies (only rice!) arriving after a few days. The aerodrome fatigue was carried on for another few days. On 1 June 1942, we were ordered to move to Buller Camp. Lt. Ajmer Singh was the camp commandant, later relieved by Lt. Col. Parkash Chand.

At Buller Camp, fatigue was not so hard. Accommodation and food were satisfactory. The Allies had suffered numerous defeats and the Germans were nearing Alexandria. Lt. Kunizuku came to us again. He said it was no use holding out any longer. Alexandria would fall any day and the Axis would overrun India soon. It was necessary to join the INA and thus establish a claim for posts in the future Government. The earlier we joined, the better; otherwise, we would lose our seniority; and those who had already joined up would supersede us.

But Buller Camp came to be noted for its anti-INA attitude. Once, when an INA dramatic troupe proceeded with songs and a drama in the midst of which words such as "Azad" were uttered, the men, suspecting that propaganda was being carried on for INA enlistment, pelted the dramatic party with stones, bricks, and so forth. In this camp too, fatigue money was not being paid. It was rumored that the INA was misappropriating the amount handed to them by the Japanese for this purpose.

The 6/1 and 8/1 men went on a hunger strike with the intention of bringing their promises to the notice of the Japanese. Among others, their grievances were (1) No compulsion to be used in enrolling for the INA; (2) Payment of fatigue money; (3) Distinct Prisoners of War Flag.

On 1 October 1942 an order was issued that those who still refused to become volunteers would move to Selctar. We moved. The General Officer Commanding paid a visit to the camp and gave a final warning, saying that the British were our bitterest enemies and this was the time to crush them. He recalled the mutiny[12], Jallianwalla Bagh[13], the imprisonment of thousands of patriots, and exploitation. The Japanese were going to help us. If we joined them, we would be treated like brothers. If we refused, God help us — he could not say what might become of us. We would be treated as sympathizers of the enemy. One thing he was sure of: we would be made to do the hardest possible labor, with practically no food, medicine and clothing, and perhaps taken to some distant places from which we would never return. It would be dying a dog's death. He would see to it that not a single non-volunteer returned to India when peace came. If one did not join, let him remain passive, and not influence others. Anyone found influencing others would be sent to a "pleasant home" (he obviously referred to the concentration camp). For every single INA man killed, a hundred non-volunteers would be killed. We too had been laughing at his venture. But now, we could see that his army was ready and fully equipped for the task, et cetera, etc.

INA Intelligence men would roam about the camp incognito to find the slightest excuse to pounce upon their victim. Any word uttered by men against the INA was at once reported to camp commanders who were of course INA men well trained and noted for their ability to do the job.

---

[12] The Indian Mutiny of 1857, also called The Sepoy Mutiny or India's First War of Independence.

[13] The Jallianwalla Bagh Massacre, which resulted in an estimated 1,000 deaths.

Indian Commissioned Officers deprived of all their belongings — even badges of rank — were removed one by one to the Separation Camp, where they had to pay the penalty for their non-cooperation. Then the Viceroy's Commissioned Officers, and even senior Non Commissioned Officers and civilian clerks, were thrown into the torture camp. Some died; some were removed to hospitals; and others, unable to bear further torments, agreed to become volunteers.

On 25 December 1942, we were again transferred to River Valley Road Camp, which had previously been occupied by Australian prisoners. This camp was to be a purely Prisoners of War camp under the direct control of the Japanese. All the men were overjoyed at the thought that here at least they would be free from the INA shadow. The boundaries of the camp were marked with barbed wire entanglements, with sentries posted. Nobody could go out without a Japanese pass, except for fatigue, which was led by the Japanese. The administration of the camp was handed over to Captain G. Shenoy, an INA man, whereas the actual command rested with a Japanese lieutenant who was putting up in a bungalow close by. All the available men were being taken on fatigue. But, as there were amenities such as canteen and fatigue money and exemption from work in case of illness, the men were not put to great hardship. The quantity of rice supplied was quite ample. No INA man was allowed to enter the camp. The men were paid twenty cents a day fatigue money and spent this amount in purchasing vegetables, fruits etc., from the canteen. I was put under the Viceroy's Commissioned Officer category and was given fatigue once every week or five days. As I was in-charge of a party of fifty to hundred men, I was getting fatigue pay of $10 per month.

In the INA, a tug of war was going on between Rash Behari Bose, President of the Indian Independence League, Far East, and Mohan Singh as to who was to be the head of the INA. Mohan Singh had sent some units to Burma without the prior authority of the Indian Independence League and had refused to send them where the President wanted. It was also heard that Mohan Singh refused to despatch INA troops to China and certain other war areas, as demanded by the Japanese.

Rash Behari Bose had immense influence in Nippon. He had escaped to Japan thirty years ago and was on the British blacklist for political activities. He had married a Japanese woman and one of his sons, Nakamura, was in the Emperor's Forces.

Owing to this disagreement, Rash Behari Bose ordered the arrest of Mohan Singh. The latter had already left instructions to all his officers to the effect that in the event of his arrest, the INA should be considered as automatically dissolved and all records pertaining to it destroyed. The INA soldiers were at liberty to revert to their Prisoner-of-War status.

Col. JNRB was appointed "General Officer in Command" of the second INA, Rash Behari Bose himself being the ex-officio Supreme Commandant. A pamphlet was printed in Roman-Urdu script detailing the causes leading to the dissolution of the First INA. A mention was also made regarding the concentration camp, which existed without the knowledge of the Japanese or Mr. Subhash Chandra Bose. Mr. Bose was aghast to hear of the atrocities committed on fellow-Indians there, and ordered the immediate closing down of the "separation camp." He gave instructions that no coercion should be used and that those who had joined the first INA were at liberty to leave it if the conditions of the 2nd INA did not suit them. The conditions of the 2nd INA were to "volunteer for service unconditionally, to free India, and to carry out the orders of superior officers."

In February/March 1943, enlistment in the 2nd INA started. No coercion was used this time, but it was more or less made clear that those who did not volunteer would be taken away by the Japanese out of Malaya for fatigue purposes and put to extreme, life-threatening hardship.

The only Red Cross amenity we received during our entire captivity was a peg of brandy and six ounces of milk on 1 January 1943. The brandy issued by the Japanese was of the Chinese type, a very inferior liquid evidently substituted for a

27

good quality one from India. Only one letter written in October 1942 was received by me in April 1943. It was rumored that Red Cross comforts were received in sufficient quantity but were eaten up by the hungry Japanese — and what was left, by the INA men.

SHIPPED OUT OF MALAYA

The first batch of approximately five hundred men for fatigue overseas was selected from Adam Road and Paya Lebar Road Camps. This batch, along with a large number of Japanese, left in early December 1942, and was torpedoed and sunk by an American submarine off the North Coast of New Guinea. The men had fortunately been provided with life belts, and floated in the water for nearly three days. The submarine would appear on the surface and machine gun the floating men who shouted "Indian Prisoners!" It was hardly likely that the submarine's personnel heard this, since the submarine came up again and again to machine gun the unfortunate victims. Many died from machine-gunning, exposure, and fear. On the third day a Japanese cruiser appeared and picked up the Japanese first, and then those prisoners who were able to swim to the cruiser, and made off — leaving the rest to their fate. The men who were fortunate enough to get into the cruiser were given a severe thrashing by the Japanese for shouting out that they were Indians. Out of five hundred, more than half the number perished in the Pacific Ocean. Mr. Shivmal of Bantwal was among the victims, as were some bakers of the 12 FB (Chhotu, Abdul Rashid, etc.).

The crew landed the men at Pilan, where they were detained for treatment for about a month, arriving in New Britain in February 1943.

The second batch of one thousand men comprising remnants of miscellaneous units left RVR Camp during January 1943 and arrived in Rabaul within twenty days. They were given the work of unloading and stacking supplies from steamers. It appears this party was treated comparatively better. Although put to hard work, they were given sufficient rations including tinned fish, milk, and so on. This party was in-charge of Jemadar Gomal Singh of Mechanical Transport.

The third batch ("San Chutai" in Japanese) to go out was ours. Some Japanese officers came to our camp in early March 1943 and wanted a fatigue party. The destination was not known. Some thought it might be for Formosa, or Java-Sumatra for sugar manufacturing work. Excitement ran high, and everyone who got a place in this batch was considered lucky. Anyhow, all those who did not join the INA had to leave Singapore, and so why not leave earlier? Five hundred and thirty of us were handed by the Camp Commandant, Lt. Kesar Singh, to the Japanese officer Lt. Yokokawa, and clothing was issued. A last warning was given that anyone desirous of getting out of this detail could do so by volunteering for the INA. At the handing over ceremony, Kesar Singh crudely put it that we would be given "civil work". Did this mean we were to be set free and given the status of civilians or asked to run the civil government in any Japanese occupied territory? Anyway, it appeared that we could be better off. The men were overjoyed at getting out of the clutches of the INA even if it meant an unknown fate.

THE TORTURE SHIP

We were marched off from the camp on 1 April 1943, and rested in the harbor godown. We saw a very large number of Indian prisoners already collected there ready to leave Singapore. So, after all we were not alone. This thought relieved our temporary dejection. At midnight, we were ordered to embark on Cargo Vessel No. 369, of hardly 800 - 900 tons. Each hold was divided into two by planks fitted to the hold, so that two compartments — each three feet in height — were made of one hold; one could enter or come out of the compartment only by crawling. We were packed inside like cattle. The space available to each man was hardly three feet long and one foot broad so that it was impossible to sleep there. Approximately two thousand men including about two hundred Japanese were squeezed in, although the Japanese occupied the top holds and did not suffer like us. Other troops accompanying us were the 1st Hyderabad Battalion, Indian State Forces, The Hong Kong Singapore Royal Artillery, and The Bahawalpurs.

Added to the congestion inside was the intense heat from the nearby boiler — and suffocation, darkness, and stench. Could Inferno be worse? The engines rattled and the "Torture Ship" crawled out of the harbor at midday on 2 April, 1943.

Slowly and more slowly it sailed on, heading for the south, and our ordeal worsened as hours passed. Heat, suffocation, stench, thirst. We were allowed a handful (hardly two ounces) of cooked rice and a little dry fish and a cup of water twice daily. The Japanese said if we ate more in the ship, we would fall ill as we were not doing any fatigue. We did not worry much about the quantity of food. We would not have minded even if we were not given any; but with the two cups of water supplied per day, one might die of thirst. We tried to go on the deck to have a breath of fresh air for which we longed so much; but the moment we climbed up the staircase, we would be kicked down by the Japanese sentries. There was no question of a bath or wash, although plenty of sea water was available on the deck. Why were the Japanese treating us like this? Because we had not joined the INA? The Japanese would torture us to death in this manner, then throw us into the deep seas.

Our ordeal was enlivened when, on 4 May 1943, the Japanese issued envelopes to each man and asked for stools. Owing to lack of food, water, and air, it was hardly possible for even the healthiest man to pass a free motion. Therefore, to collect within a few hours envelopes from two thousand men to whom only half dozen latrines were allowed, was impossible. As the envelopes were not handed over at the prescribed hour, the Japanese got enraged and started thrashing the medical officers. Finally, the envelopes were collected by the Japanese, and as some confusion occurred in numbering or recording the results, the scheme was abandoned that day; and our medical officers were ordered to get envelopes filled again the next day. To a sensible man, it would have been apparent that it was quite impossible for a normal individual to pass stools within the next twelve hours after starving from hunger and thirst. But there was no arguing with the Japanese. So, our officers had a brainwave. They asked the men to pay something to the sweeper, who would be quite willing to fill up their envelopes in a couple of hours from the stools in the latrine. And the Japanese were well pleased as the envelopes were handed to them in time. When the carrier test was conducted however, some men who were quite fit were declared to be suffering from dysentery, and those who were actually dysentery cases were declared fit as the sweeper had kindly enclosed a fit man's stools in their envelopes. And so, the "unfit" men were detained in Sourabaya and the "fit" taken.

On 6 May 1943, we arrived in Sourabaya, Java, and before noon we were asked to disembark. We camped just near the harbor and were allowed to bathe in the swimming pool (Sourabaya Zwembad-Haven). To be free again, at any rate for the time being, to have a good bath and inhale as much fresh breeze as we wished, was like being in heaven. The Javanese brought fruit and eggs for sale at exceedingly cheap rates. I bought 30 eggs for a Malayan dollar (Re.1/9 annas) and 4 plantains a cent.

Would we be kept in Sourabaya? If so, we would think ourselves well compensated for our troubles. We were lying in the open; the blue sky and the charming scenery around made us forget our troubles for the time being.

Malay soldiers, who had previously formed part of the Dutch Army in Java and Sumatra, catered to us and were very kind.

The next day, the Japanese called some of the senior Indian Officers and asked whether Indian Prisoners would like to join the Japanese and fight the British. Malay soldiers were helping them; but if we did not, all of us might be shot.

Our officers replied that Indian prisoners would be quite willing to do any kind of manual work, but would not under any circumstances fight the British. On hearing this, the Japanese are said to have beaten the colonel of the 1st Hyderabad Regiment. We were then issued with Dutch army uniforms — green coat, trousers, hat, "puffies," mess tins etc. The Japanese insisted that we wear that uniform, but our officers agreed to the use of the Dutch green coat only, since they suspected that the Japanese were trying to enlist us.

THE SECOND VOYAGE OF THE TORTURE SHIP

On the morning of 8 May 1943, nearly 500 Malays, natives of Celebes who happened to be former soldiers in the Dutch Army, embarked on our ship; after which, all Indians were ordered to board. Our hopes were again dashed to the ground. So, after all, we were not stopping in Sourabaya. Where could they be taking us? Perhaps the Malay soldiers would be able to give us an inkling.

The steamer sailed south again. The Malays are a nice people, very polite and sociable. They pitied the Indians. The Malays were given better rations and accommodation. They told us we were nearing Bali Island. Some of them were seniors and could tell us the location of the ship by merely looking at the waves. After a two-day run south, the steamer changed its direction to north-northeast. Were they taking us to Celebes or to the Philippines? The Malays said this could not be, Celebes was their home.

The pangs of hunger and thirst again seized us; heat and stench increased. Owing to the intake of the Malays, it was only with the greatest of difficulty that we could get a cup of water. For twenty-four hours each day, we were confined in those cells to suffocate and sweat. I would often go to the Malays for a cup of water; and if I got one, I would consider myself very lucky. At nighttime, I would thirst as if in the throes of last agony and then lift the water-bottle to my lips. Even a drop that trickled down was so precious. It soothed my parched lips for the time being.

Could humanity be degraded to such an extent? Could Providence be as cruel? The steamer had only one kitchen from which water was being rationed, and the two thousand men had to come one after the other, in a line, for that cup of life-preserving liquid. The rush began at 6 AM. My turn came at about 10 AM, after four hours of waiting, only to be met with the curt words, "Water finished!" Heavens, what was I to do until next day? Who knows? Before I could reach the front of the line, water might be exhausted again next day? Death was certain. I went round with a cup to my Indian friends, to Malays, even to Japanese, and was met with the reply "Sorry, I have very little." That day passed.

The next day I got up early, but the crowd had already collected. It would take three hours before my turn came. My throat was entirely dry. I could not speak. I sat on the deck at a distance with my water bottle and a cup in hand thinking to myself: I hear that in this war many ships have been sunk. Why does not an Allied submarine or plane come and sink this rotten ship too? My parched body would feel cool in the blue waters of the ocean if only for a moment, and then my sufferings would be over — once and for all . . . . While I was in this mood, a pipe in front of me sprang a leak and water sprouted. I rushed to the spot and tasted a drop. It was fresh water. Oh God, it was so sweet! At once I filled my bottle, and with the cup drank as much as my stomach could hold, going away satisfied and contented. I felt sure Providence had come to my rescue and saved me from death. I thought this was one of the happiest days of my life. By this time, a large crowd had gathered and was struggling to collect the wasting water. The man who could collect one bottle of it was considered very lucky.

At this time, another calamity overtook us. Dysentery broke out on the ship. The few latrines were being used by both unfit and fit men. In our own party of one hundred and fifty, three or four deaths occurred daily. The corpses were wrapped in a worn-out blanket and lowered into the deep ocean, unwept for and unsung. I could see hardy men prostrate with dysentery, unable to move, without any clothes. The Japanese did not pay any heed to what was going on. Dysentery spread to other holds of the ship, killing seven to eight daily. But the ship was not stopped, nor was an attempt made to evacuate the victims.

Insanitation and squalor increased. There had been cases of men dying from dysentery within a day of getting sick. Commotion increased. What was going to happen? Our officers requested the Japanese that the suffering men might be disembarked at one of the neighboring islands, but they evaded action by saying, "Mo Sukoshi" ["a little more", meaning in this context: have patience for just a little longer]. Except for separate accommodation being allowed, no treatment was given to the men, and the disease spread anyway. The scene was pitiful and heart-rending. Brave, virile soldiers who would have defied anybody in battle were now helpless like babies and were groaning and rolling naked on the floor presenting a weird spectacle. I could not bear it and tears started trickling from my eyes as nothing in my life had moved me to that extent. Was this the penalty we were paying for being honest and principled?

The torture ship continued careening nonchalantly north, northeast, north, northeast, unmindful of the tragedy that was being enacted in its own bowels. Was it possible we were being taken to the Philippines? "Not likely," our Malay friends replied, "maybe perhaps Palau." They were right. To our left and to our right we could see at a distance islands abounding in jungles and hills. On 22 May 1943, the thirteenth day of sailing from Sourabaya, we reached Palau.[14]

---

[14] A small island country in the Western Pacific, east of the Philippines and somewhat to the north of the Western part of the island of New Guinea.

This was a Japanese base. We could see a large number of cruisers, destroyers, submarines, and transport vessels around. This island had originally belonged to the Germans, but was handed over to the Japanese after the First World War for their service to the Allies.

To our great relief, our ship anchored there. We thought our troubles were over at last. But this was not to be. A week passed without any news. Dysentery patients were not disembarked; deaths occurred daily. We were again in suspense. We hoped we might be allowed more fresh water and better food, but were soon disillusioned.

On the 12th day of our arrival, we were ordered to get ready for disembarkation. The Hong Kong Singapore Royal Artillery was the first to receive these orders. Over two hundred of our men had disembarked when we were ordered to stop disembarkation and told that the men already in the island would be returning. The two hundred men were allowed to have a bath on the island, and returned to the ship after one hour. They told us the island had good roads. Indian prisoners were already there, including 400 men of the 1st Hyderabad Regiment. They said they were given hard fatigue but sufficient food.

Another week passed. It seemed that the Japanese had no definite plans for us and were awaiting instructions. Corpses of men who died on the ship were now allowed to be taken to the island for burial.

Another request was made to the Japanese to disembark the ailing men, but was met with the same reply "Mo sukoshi - fu nichi - jotho kai kai" meaning "Ten days more, and you will be given good food".

The steamer now took the southern direction — south, southeast, south, southeast. Were we going to New Guinea? Australia? The Malays came to our rescue again. "Rabaru," they said. Where the hell could this be? We had never heard of such a place before. Rabaru? It turned out the Malays were right again. We were being taken to the now famous Rabaul, capital of New Britain.[15]

This time however, we were allowed three cups of water daily and were also allowed to go on the decks for fresh air. We were given a seawater bath by having a hose turned upon us: That was a great boon, a bath after one and a half months! But the ordeal of the journey was already telling on us. Two or three men died daily, and their corpses were unceremoniously lowered into the deep waters of the Pacific.

On the 26th morning, we arrived in Kokopo, a port 30 miles from Rabaul, and were ordered to disembark. The steamer touched at the docks, and we climbed down by means of a rope ladder hanging steeply at the ship's side. We were taken half a mile away to a place thick with bushes and jungle grass and were asked to build our own accommodation.

---

[15] New Britain is the largest island of the Bismarck Archipelago, in the southwestern Pacific and east of the island of New Guinea. About the size of Taiwan, and politically a part of Papua New Guinea at present, New Britain was mandated to Australia after World War I and taken by the Japanese in 1942.

TORTURE ISLAND

In New Britain, there is no fixed rainy season. The average annual rainfall is about eighty inches. It may rain at any time on any day of the year. So we were at a loss to find materials for our huts; and, in any case, until the huts were built, we had to have some protection from the rain. The Japanese did not give us any tentage. So we made use of ground sheets or even blankets and made a shelter. The rains came: we were all drenched, our clothing, bedding and everything. Added to this was the damp ground on which we rested. On disembarkation, we were not allowed to rest. We were made to unload the ship's cargo, which took us several hours. The next day, we were building huts from coconut palms, bamboo, and grass. Men who had never climbed a tree were compelled to climb coconut trees and were severely beaten on being unable to do so. Rice was cooked by the Japanese themselves and rationed; and although the quantity was sufficient, no curry was given, except for some salty soup of some black leaves. These leaves, already dried, bloated on immersion in water, and were then cut into pieces and cooked with salt. They were quite tasteless, and we started wondering how the Japanese could relish it.

Owing to rain, wet clothing and bedding, and mosquitoes, an acute form of malaria broke out. Even the patients, although kept separately, were left in the open without a roof over their heads. There they lay shivering and uncared for, only quinine being given to them and a little rice! The Japanese said patients must eat little as they were not doing fatigue.

I had an attack of malaria in the first week of July 1943. I could not get even a drop of hot water. There on the ground I lay, shivering, helpless. The thin cotton blanket given to me being inadequate to protect me from the cold, I waited for the sun to warm me. I would shiver like a leaf. Then, seized by fever, my body would turn as hot as fire — I would become unconscious, then awake only to find myself perspiring. There was not a soul who could give a sip of even cold water. I could not blame them as all the fit men had been away taken for work and the ailing left to their fate.

Our "Senior Medical Officer," a Subedar Raja Singh, was a brute of a man. He had not an iota of mercy. He would shout and growl at the patients for no reason at all. One day it happened that the crowd at the Medical Inspection Room was too large. My condition was such that I could neither stand nor sit. I lay down, and as I had high temperature, I become unconscious. In half an hour, I regained consciousness and remembered the sick parade. I dragged myself there to find my name had already been called out.

"Why are you late?" growled Raja Singh.

I explained to him that I had had high temperature, and had fallen down unconscious; that was why I had been late. He then asked me whether I was a "Madrasi".[16] I said yes. "You seem to be all right now. You can go for fatigue." And so saying, he sent me away. Owing to my powerless condition, I could not answer him. But the thought passed my mind that not even the Japanese would have been so cruel.

Raja Singh harassed several others too, especially educated men. The Japanese had selected the right type of man, I

---

[16] A derogatory term used by many North Indians to describe all South Indians, numbering a few hundred million in all, most of whom do not, and could not, come from the single city of Madras. A comparable equivalent might be if Scots were to refer to all natives of England as Londoners.

thought. This gentleman could only do one thing, and that was exempt the sick from fatigue. Even this he did not do in my case. More will be written about him later.

The construction of the huts proceeded. The Malay soldiers were quite smart and had specialized in this type of work. Three huts were constructed, one for each section. These were built in such a hurry that when we got into these, the roofs were leaking, the ground was moist, and at high tide, sea water would enter. Ants, mosquitoes, flies, and earthworms became our companions. This was the rest and the good food promised to us by the Japanese.

Out of five hundred and thirty prisoners, nearly sixty had died from dysentery during the voyage. And of the remaining, at least two hundred were suffering from malaria and dysentery.

On 21 July 1943, the fit men (roughly two hundred and fifty) were moved to Rabaul thirty miles from the camps. We were taken there in launches.

Rabaul was the capital of New Britain. In pre-Japanese days, it was administered by the Australian Government, having been mandated to them by the Allies after the First World War. The island originally belonged to the Germans and was known as "Nau Frau" in the Bismarck Archipelago. Rabaul in the Kanaka language means "Place of Mangroves" and is known as the "Naples of the East."

At this place, too, the problem of accommodation presented itself: "Build your huts as you go." The Japanese were a practical people. They never worried about food or accommodation. "Eat whatever you get and sleep wherever there is place," was their slogan. A space of three spans was available for each person.

The next day, heavy fatigue started. Cargo ships carrying supplies and ammunition were arriving and had to be unloaded. Our batch was unloading. Party Number 2, which had arrived in January, were stacking. Hand carts were used for the purpose. The Japanese soldiers loaded the carts; we carried them to the dump; and the other party stacked them methodically. We heard from them that they received sufficient food, although fatigue was hard. The Americans had been bombing them often, and now they were used to it. A big air raid had taken place in April, destroying warships and several buildings in the town. A section of theirs (about two hundred men, mostly "Madrasis") had to proceed to New Guinea for fatigue, but hardly eighty men returned alive. The rest died on account of disease and hunger. The in-charge of the N.G. Party Mr. M. Raghavendra Rao, RIASC, died of malaria in New Guinea.

Our unloading work continued in shifts, day and night.

Food was the same type as before. We were given sufficient rice twice daily, whereas the Malays and the Japanese got it thrice. In September, we were also given rice thrice, but the trouble was with the curry. The same thick black leaves, soaked in water, cut, and boiled, formed our curry. Nobody ate it. We were feeling hungry after hard work, but how to swallow the rice? We bought chillies and along with chilli-water or coconut, we ate the rice.

This continued for nearly two months. On 12 October 1943 at about 8 AM, while we were at work, sirens and repeated alarms of approaching enemy planes were given. [Editor's note: by "enemy" the author means the Allies — who, ironically, have now become "the enemy" to be feared for one's life.]

"Kekaikeho" was the signal given as a warning if the planes were thought to be in the vicinity. "Khushu" meant "actual danger" and was given when the planes were approaching the island. It often happened that, after Kekaikeho was sounded, the planes took some other direction and disappeared without flying over the island. In such a case, the Khusho was not sounded. On this occasion, however, hardly had the echoes of the first warning died down when the second alarm was given! Panic ensued. The Japanese started running helter-skelter, the Malays and Indians following. We ran for our lives as fast as our legs could carry us. A Malay soldier who was with me wanted to take shelter in a huge supply dump.

I abused him saying that the dump would be the first target to be hit and so we ran and ran until we reached the top of a hill a mile or two away, where we sat down exhausted.

The raiders came in large numbers, about three to four hundred I should think, and started pounding the town, the harbor, the dumps, the warships, and anything they could lay their bombs on. We could clearly see the bombs drop and hear the terrific explosions. Some dumps of petrol and other inflammable material caught fire, sending clouds of smoke into the skies. The earth trembled, even the hill on which we took shelter trembled. Was the Day of Judgement approaching? We waited patiently. The raiders disappeared for a while, another batch came and continued pounding, a third one appeared relieving the second, and so on. The bombing continued for an hour, after which the planes flew away.

We then made for our lines to find everybody in the heat of excitement running here and there like madmen, their faces horror-stricken. I asked them what the matter was, and if there were casualties. They simply muttered, "Our men are buried in trenches." I went to the spot to find men feverishly digging a trench which had collapsed, burying the unfortunate men taking shelter. A huge bomb had fallen a couple of yards from this trench: some corpses had already been dug out, their eyes glassy, mouths open with mud inside, presenting a ghastly sight. They had tried to scoop out the mud with their hands, feet and mouth in an attempt to free themselves, but had died in extreme agony; more bodies were dug out bringing the total to twenty-seven to thirty men. Rescue work could not proceed until the planes had actually vanished, and then it was too late.

The spectacle outside was equally gruesome. Warships and transport vessels had disappeared into the sea, some leaning on the waves as if drunk. Supply dumps were burning, skeletons of godowns and sheds were left. The town was burning. Huge bombs had made craters as deep as ten feet and thirty to forty feet in diameter, water sprouting from these craters.

Some cargo ships were still left standing, so the unloading continued the next day. An air raid alarm was again given, and the men ran. The raiders this time pounded the aerodrome ten to fifteen miles away and left. When the "all clear" signal was given, work was continued — unloading, clearing debris, repairing roads, and salvage. This routine continued, American planes appearing punctually every morning, hitting targets here and there, then disappearing. The Japanese air strength was too weak at this time to oppose the Americans, who were left a free hand.

On the early morning of 5 November 1943, Japanese transports brought fresh reinforcements of troops known as the "Taiwan Brigade," and disembarkation commenced. The American Intelligence Service had apparently been too vigilant, for formations of bombers appeared from nowhere. Incessant air raid alarms were given and everyone was ordered to take shelter. The new arrivals, following the Indians, rushed to whatever trench was available. I took shelter in one of the two trenches adjacent to our huts. The American planes started raining bombs everywhere; our huts were aflame. How could we get out and salvage our things? The raiders were still active. After they had gone, we rushed to our barracks to find all our belongings reduced to ashes. One bomb had dropped exactly over our trench, collapsing the second trench only three to four yards away. Other trenches down below had also collapsed, also the two trenches involved in the first disaster.

Rescue work started. Everyone who was dug out had died. Several men standing outside the trench were mortally hit by splinters and dismembered, some losing arms, legs, and having their stomachs ripped open. Some breathed their last after being dug out. The Taiwanese dug out hundreds of their comrades but finding it impossible to take out every one, left the rest in the collapsed trench, Nature's own grave.

This disaster was even more terrible than the first. We lost twenty-five men. The Taiwanese, who had arrived that morning only to die in Rabaul, lost several hundreds. We buried the Indians quietly, but the Japanese went away, leaving the corpses strewn on roads. There they lay for nearly four days. We had to pass by them every now and then. The Japanese didn't even care for their dead. The decomposed corpses were at last removed.

We were now faced with the problem of accommodation and bathing. Nothing was left except what was on our person. The Japanese issued us with one blanket each, and some tarpaulins for the purpose of erecting shelters. These tarpaulins were badly torn and could not protect us from rain.

Until now, the Japanese had prepared trenches without exits. The mud being soft, the trenches collapsed, entrapping the men completely. From then onwards, men were afraid to take shelter in such trenches. The Japanese now commenced the construction of long trenches with an exit at the opposite side. Coconut tree trunks and planks were fitted to prevent them from collapsing.

Heavy fatigue started: building trenches and huts, laying underground cables, transporting ammunition and supplies.

At this time, an ulcer developed on my right leg, and so being unable to walk, I was despatched to Kokopo Hospital for Prisoners (under the charge of Dr. Naul Chand) for treatment. The barracks were by now all dilapidated, and only those who had ground sheets could keep themselves away from rain. I had nothing with me, and my plight was bad. The floor was moist and infested with ants, crabs, rats etc.

To add to my misery, at high tide, sea water would come right into the barrack, again dampening the ground. I had only a torn piece of blanket, which could not even protect me from mosquitoes. Hardly had my wound healed, malaria seized me again. I lay there shivering like a leaf, left to my fate. I had such a longing for a cup of hot tea that I would have even bartered my very life for it; but I could not get even a cup of hot water. At 11 AM, two thin rotis of rotten wheat were given, with no vegetable. On some days, sweet potato leaves were boiled without salt and given. That was something to satisfy our hunger. Not a grain of salt was available.

The Japanese had by now mustered their air force and were giving combat to the allied planes. The dogfights in which one or two planes would fall into the sea were worth seeing. The

Japanese said the wrecked planes were American. We thought otherwise.

THE BOMBS OF SANTA CLAUS

The 25th of December 1943, being Christmas, we thought perhaps the Allies would rest, but no. As if to greet us, happy formations of fighters were seen approaching Rabaul early in the morning, and a big battle ensued. As usual, a few planes fell into the sea. An hour's display, and the planes vanished.

At the end of December 1943 I, along with some less serious patients, was transferred to Rabaul.

In Rabaul, the few cargo ships that still survived were being unloaded, but owing to rains and consequent damage to the harbor area, the hand carts would not work. The supplies had to be carried to the stacking place. They were loaded in lorries and transported to camouflaged dumps in the interior.

In January 1944, a huge convoy of [Japanese] cruisers, destroyers, torpedo boats, cars, ships, and transport vessels arrived in New Britain waters. Some cargo ships had touched the docks. The enemy [the Allies] got wind of this. Wave after wave of bombers arrived on a fine morning and started dive-bombing the vessels. Guns barked incessantly, but no hit was scored on the raiders. The latter pounded the vessels and made for the sky, only to be relieved by another formation which, having done its job, was followed by a third. The number of planes that took part in the raid could not have been less than four to five hundred. The whole sky was darkened by the presence of these monsters. The planes departed after hours of bombing, being proud that they had achieved their object. Their pride was entirely justified for, as we surveyed the harbor, hardly a single ship was visible, and the few that could be seen were partially capsized as if mortally wounded.

Tears rolled from the eyes of some of the Japanese officers. They made a touching reference to a huge vessel which had brought tanks just the previous day, and was now at the bottom of the sea.

We were proud and very much encouraged at this. The end of the Japs was not far.

During these months, air raids were concentrated mainly on Japanese aerodromes in Rabaul, which were being bombed inch by inch. Safer trenches had now been constructed here and there. As soon as the planes appeared, we would disperse and return on the "all clear" signal.

At the end of March 1944, the raiders did not appear for nearly a week. By that time, we had new barracks built on the ashes of the old ones. Why were the planes not coming? Were negotiations for peace going on? One fine morning (2 April 1944), a large formation of raiders approached us at very great speed. We ran for our lives and hid in trenches. The planes flew very low and passed our barracks. No explosion was heard. A little later, a rumbling noise was heard, our barracks were aflame, but we did not dare to come out for fear of being detected.

When we felt certain that the planes would not return, we came out of our hiding places to find everything reduced to ashes! What a fate! The Japanese did not issue us any clothing. As outside fatigue was heavy, huts could not be rebuilt quickly. There, we lay in the open, without anything to cover us or spread under our bodies, at the mercy of the elements. All day we worked; and at night, being tired, we would try to sleep in a crouched position. The raiders would come roaring and drop their deadly load here and there.

Well! By now we had become accustomed to the bombers. They no longer scared us. Our only grievance against them was that they disturbed our sleep. Otherwise, they were welcome. Their planes were our only hope of deliverance or our end, either of which was desirable. The greater their number, the prouder we felt. They were our only salvation. A few of us (notably Mr. Harbans Lal, Sen, and I) never took shelter during the air raids, but gazed at the maneuvers in the air.

If, on any night, planes did not appear, our friend Rain made it a point of visiting us: which, to us, was far worse. We were all drenched, but where could we run? How could we sleep? The words from the Scriptures came to mind : "The bird has his nest, and the beast his den, but the Son of Man knows not where to lay his head . . . ." [Editor's note: the last two phrases were crossed out by the author in the original manuscript, as if he were unsure of the actual quote.]

Were nature and the elements conspiring against us? Work hard all day, eat meager rice, then go to sleep without a bed sheet, to find yourself awakened by the planes or rain. The torn and tattered clothes on our persons, whether wet or dry, were our only possession.

The day and night raids continued. It had become a routine. If on any day the planes did not appear, we wondered why. Was peace nearing? Were the allies contemplating a landing?

One night in May 1944, Rabaul town was heavily shelled by Allied submarines. This time, we all got into the trenches. The whole island shook. The deafening roar of the artillery and the blast of the exploding shells, I admit, made us nervous. Undoubtedly, the Allies were preparing to land, and this was the covering fire. In a few days' time, either we would be free or gone. Either option was good. Only a couple of days more, and our sufferings would be over. We planned to run away and hide in the wild jungles until the Australians rescued us. Never mind about food; by now, we had been well trained to starve and would be able to carry on without food for several days at a stretch by eating dry coconuts or raw papayas. Water was available in the streams.

Another thought struck us. In the jungle, there were Kanakas who were acting as Japanese spies. Would they not betray us? And if we were apprehended — which was not unlikely — the Japanese would behead us. And so, we gave up the idea of escape. We would rely on Providence.

The next day, no shelling took place and the Japanese were going about their business as usual. After all, the submarines were mainly playing stunts. No landing had taken place.

No steamers came now. Huge dumps of supplies had been destroyed. The Japanese would have to ration supplies, as further importation was an impossibility. There were nearly 100,000 troops to be fed and clothed in the event of a prolonged siege. The situation was gloomy. The Japanese authorities now issued orders for cultivation of the land. Tapioca was the main item. Large areas were turned into tapioca gardens. Besides, attempts were made to grow rice, maize, and vegetables. Our daily ration was reduced to hardly eight ounces of rice. At recess, some of us went in search of papayas, wild brinjal,[17] and any kind of edible grass which was boiled with or without salt, and eaten along with the meager quantity of rice.

From January, three or four batches of forty to fifty men had left us to places forty to eighty miles away for garden fatigue or construction of trenches. Only about one hundred fifty of them were left in the main camp. By this time, we had lost nearly one hundred and twenty men.

Planes did not raid in large numbers. Now, usually four three-engine bombers visited us every morning punctually at eight. Then they would disappear, leaving one on guard. We called them the four Marx Brothers. The fourth reconnoiter the whole island, preying upon any sea camp, road traffic, and so on. Sometimes, one more would join him. By lunchtime both of them departed, unloading their deadly contents either on a

---

[17] Eggplant.

lorry, a hut, a dump, or in the jungle. Two planes would return in the afternoon and disappear in the evening, with two others relieving them for the night.

On 5 July 1944 still one more tragedy occurred. Our latrine, hardly ten yards from the barrack, was overcrowded at 3 AM; and after a few minutes only 3 men were inside — Jemadar Harbans Lal, RIAS 1, Sen Gupta, Postal Service, and Lance Naik Sundar Singh, 22 Mechanical Transport Company.

It transpired that somebody in the Japanese Battalion accommodation nearby lit a cigarette. The lone raider in the sky above was alert and noticed this. He threw a grenade (some say a light bomb) on the Japanese, one on the Hyderabad Infantry and a third one right in front of the latrine. The latrine was completely blown off, and the bodies of poor Sen Gupta and Sardar Singh were scattered in fragments 30-40 yards away. It was pitch dark at that time, so no search could be made. A little later, what remained of the victims was collected.

Sen Gupta's head and thighs had been severed, Sardar Singh disemboweled, and poor Harbans Lal's skull had been cracked, his body thrown into the steel tub. These gentleman died the most cruel death imaginable.

A pit 2 to 3 feet deep and 5 to 6 feet in diameter was visible in front of the latrine. A splinter of the bomb flew towards me and came to rest on my bed as I was trying to jump out. My left middle finger came in contact with it, resulting in a slight burn. I had had a narrow escape, but my friends had not. These men could very well have stayed back in Singapore and saved their own lives, but came with the fatigue party to be away from the INA influence in vindication of certain principles.

Dark gloom was cast over the entire camp. They had been quite hale and healthy the previous night: Harbans Lal, Sen Gupta, and I had been talking till late that night, planning our postwar schemes, and now my only friends there were no more. I could not restrain myself, and tears rolled down my cheeks.

The realization dawned upon us that our lives were now not safe. On any day at any time, we too might be killed. But time is a great healer. In a fortnight, this tragic experience was almost forgotten, and we went about our business as if nothing had happened. The graveyard where our comrades were buried was only a few yards from our huts. Now, a strange feeling came over us. We thought these men to be lucky. They were dead, but their troubles were at an end. There they lay, resting in peace, quite unconcerned about the holocaust and destruction going on in the world. They died brave martyrs to their cause, having done their duty well. And we envied them!

In August 1944, planes came by in larger numbers. They approached from the south, flew over us, and disappeared. Early one morning, I was working on a garden close by with a party of ten men when a huge formation of bombers was seen approaching. All the rest ran away, but I stood still and watched the planes. Hardly had they passed over my head, than the dry grass all around me was aflame, with clouds of smoke rising. I ran to a safer place; and on returning, saw that "fire bottles" had been thrown down. One of these bottles, had it come in contact with a man, would have been sufficient to kill him. A horse fell dead as if electrocuted when a bottle fell on its body.

On 12 August 1944, I was taken to a place called Naga Naga 30-40 miles from Rabaul in order to replace a casualty. Already, fifty-four men had gone there for fatigue. Although my condition was weak owing to prolonged malaria and tropical wounds, I was not spared from work. We were taken down to the Daisan Hombu Battalion Headquarters[18] two miles away, who ordered us to do road repairing, dugouts for petrol bunks, and gardening. Although they exacted hard work, their treatment of us was not bad. They did not beat anyone, and those suffering from malaria or any other disease were given rest.

Our huts were situated in a nullah[19] for fear of detection by planes. The kitchen was a mile away. Accommodation allowed was three spaces to each man. The rice, fairly good, was not

---

[18] 3rd Division HQ.
[19] A ravine, a watercourse, not necessarily dry.

meager. We also got a curry made of a kind of leaf that is plentiful in the New Britain jungles. At recess time, we went in search of dry coconuts and chillies. The Japanese commander's name was Ootani Gunsou [Staff Sergeant Ootani]. He was not a good man. He forbade Indians to leave the hut at any time or to bring in coconuts or papayas. Search of our belongings was made frequently. We had also about ten Indonesian soldiers with us. He treated them better. Ootani was, however, kindly disposed towards the sick. He dressed wounds and gave out quinine. Our men had a strong dislike for him, which I think was not justified to that extent.

On 25 August 1944, commotion prevailed among the Japanese. Through an Indonesian, we learned that Palan had been captured by the Americans. All fit men of our party were ordered to move to a place called Kitayama forty to fifty miles away near the sea for the purpose of constructing gun implements. I, along with seven others, was left out. Our party of eight was in the charge of a sepoy named Harai Joutouhei [Private First Class Harai]. He was the kindest of all the Japanese I had met. He was a young fellow hardly thirty years old, good-natured and considerate. He used to send two or three of us by turn on fatigue which consisted of five to six hours of light garden work near the Dai Tai Hombu (Battalion HQ). The Japanese in-charge of the fatigue was also a kind man, with an amiable nature. He never ill-treated us. The Japanese officers from the HQ used to visit the garden and themselves do some work. They had a kind word for us, which we very much appreciated. An Indian's nature is such that he can easily be pleased. It is not necessary to give him things. A few kind words and courteous treatment — and he is quite satisfied. He is sentimental.

FISH AND FOWL

During these months, very little rice was being given to us — not more than six ounces daily, I should imagine. Before we went out on fatigue, cooked rice was given to us for the morning as well as noon. Papayas cooked without salt were dished out as curry. I would eat three or four spoonfuls; then, being alarmed at the disappearing quantity, muse to myself whether to eat all of it. If I ate it all, nothing would be left for the noon, when one felt hungry as a wolf after half a day's toil. If I did not, then I would remain half-hungry in the morning — and my appetite was too strong . So, I decided to eat the whole lot and go to work without anything.

11 AM was lunch time. My Japanese commander asked me where my food was. I replied that the quantity was so small that I ate the whole lot in the morning. He then asked me to go search for any coconuts. Going quickly to the neighboring Kanaka garden, I lifted a fallen coconut, broke it with a pickaxe, and ate it.

This routine continued for a few days until no more dry coconuts were left. So I did not eat in the mornings and kept the whole lot of four ounces of rice for the noon meal, so that I could have one "good" meal at least. After a few days, this procedure was reversed.

One day, I had eaten the whole quantity of rice in the morning. No coconuts were available in the neighboring gardens. The Japanese were rearing poultry as well. The fowls were in need of coconut, too. A Japanese resident and I went in search of coconuts for the fowls. We wandered for three to four miles, succeeded in collecting twenty coconuts, and returned. The Japanese scraped two, mixed in some sesame leaves (Doilori pappa), and asked me to feed the chickens. As I was feeding the chickens, my heart sank. For I was feeling hungry, too. I wished I could have eaten the feed myself. I would have done so had the Japanese not been watching me.

In the middle of November, a lorry-load of condemned tinned fish was thrown near our garden, the intention being to use the fish as manure for the garden. That day, one of our men brought home two tins. We opened them. Although old and unfit for consumption in the normal course, to us it tasted just fine. Our companions said there was a huge dump of them near our garden. Hurrah, our joy knew no bounds! An oasis had been found in the wilderness. We would now not starve. Providence had come to our rescue. Whether good or bad, it mattered little. We might die of food poisoning, but not of hunger, the former being preferable. The next day I brought in a sack full of these tins. We opened them and ate the contents. Some of them had turned sour. I knew well that it would harm us. My companions asked for my opinion. I told them the fish was quite good, only that the sauce had turned it sour! And so we consumed four or five one-pound tins daily. It did not matter now whether the Japanese gave us any rice or not.

More quantities were brought in daily and consumed. In a month's time, the Japanese supervisor noticed that the dump had receded. He asked me who might have taken the fish. I made him understand we never touched it as we knew it was bad and sure to cause dysentery. I suggested perhaps the Kanakas who were passing by might have stolen them. He did not suspect us and told me to shift the remaining tins right inside the garden, so that the Kanakas might not steal.

The Japanese then asked me to cut open the tins and collect the contents in a drum. This was the type of work I was longing for. While opening the tins, I hid a few thought to be edible in the bushes close by. Most of the tins gave horrible smells indicating that the contents had deteriorated. When the Japanese had gone for lunch, I placed the hidden tins in my mess tin and took them home in the evening.

Not a grain of salt was available anywhere. Our curry of papaya and jungle leaves was cooked without salt, but with the sour fish mixed in, it tasted delicious.

I wish to record the names of the people who gave me considerable help as regards food, vegetables, and so forth during these months. Suraj Din, Giyat, IAOC, Franors, Indian Army Ordnance Corps, Ramaswamy and [illegible] of MT. I had my Christmas dinner on 25 December 1944 with these gentlemen. A small anaemic fowl had been cooked in coconut milk with brinjals and tapioca. We got a bone each.

At the end of December, a further batch of fifteen men joined us. The quantity of rice was now reduced to hardly four to five ounces daily. The Japanese said they could not help it. Supply ships had all been sent off by the evening; and when more came along, we would be given plenty to eat. I faced New Year's Day, 1 January 1945, quite hungry. Thinking that my hunger would vanish in the oblivion that sleep brought, I slept the whole day, forgetting everything. That was a sort of happiness: sleep and oblivion.

On the morning of 5 January 1945, five of us were ordered to go to Kita Yama for tapioca fatigue. This batch of five consisted of the weakest men in the whole group, and I feared something worse was going to happen.

We were taken in a lorry with one month's rice ration. Owing to the vigilance of the reconnaissance planes, our lorry was driven slowly, halting at the sound of a plane. To make matters worse for us, rain came and drenched us as the lorry was uncovered. We had no change of clothes, and even the torn piece of blanket that I had was wet. We shivered in the lorry, but the driver said nothing could be done. One of my companions developed acute malaria. Still, nothing could be done. On the third day, we were taken to a place where ten Japanese soldiers were staying. We were introduced to them. They said they were expecting us. No spare accommodation was available, so we must build our own huts! What, again?

With their help, we erected four pillars and a roof of coconut leaves within a couple of hours. A sort of platform two feet from the ground was erected with trunks of small trees on which to sleep. Rain came and drenched our already wet clothes and our shelter. The roof could not protect us.

The next morning, we were taken to the tapioca gardens by a Japanese soldier. He was educated and knew a little English. We were given carving knives and asked to clear grass plants grown in the gardens. Wild grass, plants, creepers, and touch-me-nots had to be cleared. We went there at 6 AM and were asked to work till 8 AM. We were allowed twenty minutes' rest and then started again. This was a hard job, bending all the time to the level of the ground and cutting the wild growth till our backs ached. We asked the Japanese to give us more rest. He said it could not be done as large areas had to be cleared.

KOGA THE DEVIL

The next day, another Japanese soldier, Koga Hugcho, was put in charge of us. I call him Koga the Devil. I still cannot forget his Satanic face nor forget his atrocities. If anyone deserves to be hanged first for the ill-treatment of prisoners, it is he. A man of about 30 years, quite well-built, with slant eyes and an ape's mouth with a gold tooth, he looked like a mixture of Japanese and Chinese, a most unprincipled and inhumane brute. Although he said he belonged to Tokyo, I am inclined to think he was either a Taiwanese or a Manchurian. The next three months that we passed with him were the bitterest of our lives. Our daily routine was: rise at 4 AM, go to the surrounding jungle and fetch two or three loads of firewood; breakfast (two spoonfuls of rice) at 5.30, off to the tapioca garden at 6 AM, cut grass till 11 with half an hour's break, return for lunch; half an hour's break, again off to the garden, back by 4 PM; fill a fifty-five gallon drum with water and boil it ready for our master's bath; again collect two or three loads of firewood. Thus were we kept busy from before daybreak to sunset. In addition, each of us was called upon by him to help the Japanese cook in preparing the morning food — in which case, we were required to get up at 2 AM. Fire had to be lit to boil rice, curry and water.

The firewood was invariably damp and gave out clouds of smoke, completely blinding our eyes. If the fire was not lighted, the Japanese cook would curse us and even beat us. Food had to be ready before daybreak so that the raiders might not notice the smoke. By now, the planes had no targets left. They would watch for any signs of smoke and let go their deadly bombs.

During fatigue, if Koga thought our speed was not up to his expectations, he would beat us with sticks, fists, and kicks. He said that Indians, like the British, were lazy and were not fit to live. They knew only to enjoy. That is why they were being defeated. He told us the Allied Navy had been completely annihilated near Formosa and in the Philippines. Land fighting was going on in the latter place, and the Japanese were winning. There was no chance of our returning to India. We would remain there in New Britain and cultivate tapioca.

In the evenings, even in heavy rain, the Japanese made us boil water for their bath. This was almost an impossibility as the fireplace and firewood became wet. But there was no argument with our masters.

Our hut was more like a pandal. Even in a light rain, water trickled inside. It was infested with rats, mosquitoes, ants, lizards and snakes. Had the Japanese given us half a day's rest, we could have improved it, but even on our so called holidays, they made us collect coconuts and extract oil for them!

I had a relapse of malaria. Koga allowed me rest as long as my temperature was on; but as soon as he felt my forehead cool, he would ask me to work. To make matters worse, an ulcer appeared on my right foot. The wound broadened, giving out pus and a horrible smell. The leg swelled, and I could not walk. No arrangement was made for dressing the wound. Not even a piece of linen was given. I tore my langoti[17], dressed the ulcer in filthy water from the nullah, and bandaged it in a dirty rag. Flies swarmed around the wound. Blood trickled down sometimes. The Japanese saw this, but were not moved with compassion. Koga said it was a trifling thing and asked me to go on fatigue. I could only walk with the help of crutches.

Other Japanese who saw me on the way thought I deserved rest.

Owing to agonizing pain, my temperature did not subside. I and the four others requested Koga to shoot us as it was better to die than to remain as their prisoners. He jokingly gave us shovels and spades, asking us to prepare our own graves so that we might be shot the next morning.

Basanta was the one most cruelly mistreated. For some trifling offence, he was tied with live battery wires; and when the unfortunate man cried for mercy, all the Japanese laughed. He fell down. They kicked him and made him get up, again tying him up with the torturing wires. Besides Basanta, there was another Sikh, Kartar Singh, with us. Koga ordered them to shave off their beards as, according to them, the beards made them ill. For disobeying him, they were beaten.

One day, Basanta was standing by. Koga, like a dog, came upon him and passed urine on him. On another occasion, Basanta was spat upon.

We again pleaded with Koga to shoot us all. He warned us not to repeat this request. We were their prisoners and must obey them. Even the British General Percival was being ordered about by a Japanese soldier. We had been defeated in the war and must not speak anything out of the way.

Koga delighted in making us work in the rain. Sometimes, he would ask us to bring grasshoppers for his fowls. If we failed to fetch the required number within the specified time, he would punish us.

Foolshah caught malaria while on fatigue one day. He had high temperature. I requested Koga to give the man rest. But Koga was Koga. He made Foolshah stand in the sun with arms outstretched and kicked him until he fainted.

In February 1945, the Ginso [Staff Sergeant] of our Buthai paid us a visit and was apparently moved to see our condition. His party was only two miles away, and he asked us to come to him for medicine. We went there during the afternoon recess. Our ulcers were being dressed weekly, but as for malaria, a decoction prepared from some strange leaves was given to the patients.

My physical condition at this stage was extremely bad. My body had become very thin. When I walked a few yards, I felt giddy and close to fainting. My weight then could not have been more than 100 pounds.

My companions and I were now very dejected. Was Providence planning to kill us slowly? Why did not we die like the others, from bombardment or disease? Our troubles would have been over. This was the limit of human endurance and degradation: hard work with practically no food or clothing, no medicine, and torture on the top of it. Of one thing, we felt certain; things could not go on indefinitely at this rate. Our deliverance or end was nearing.

In the middle of March, we were relieved and asked to join the Youchutai (two miles away). Our deliverance had come at last. We did not mind what else was in store for us. We had gotten out from the clutches of these brutes, anyhow. We thanked God for this mercy.

The new place, although not to be called comfortable, seemed so when compared to the hell from which we had just escaped. Sufficient rice was given, and sufficient rest to patients. The barracks, as was the case everywhere, were leaking. Hardly had we passed fifteen days, when five of us were taken to a place called Ditappan, thirty miles away, and attached to an Indian party of twenty-five men in-charge of Meena Gunsou [Staff Sergeant Meena] and his assistant Ishida Joutouhei [Private First Class Ishida].

Meena, like Harai, was an extremely considerate and amiable man. He knew how, when, and to whom to be lenient. He had a fair education, knew a smattering of English, and had a liking for India. The Battalion HQ officers to whom we were attached for duty were rather nasty. And Meena's hands were therefore tied. All the fit men were taken to trench fatigue, and the remaining, about ten persons including myself, were given the work of coconut scraping. Our men said trench fatigue was hard and the supervising staff rude. The Japanese Non-

Commissioned Officer in charge of the ten of us was a nice man. He asked us to scrape as many coconuts as possible till evening and dismissed us punctually at four. We did fifty to sixty coconuts.

Our daily ration now consisted of hardly 2 - 3 ounces of rice mixed with 2 - 3 ounces of boiled sweet potatoes. Curry was again of the jungle leaf variety, boiled, of course, without salt. We felt as hungry as wolves the whole day. I thought myself extremely lucky to be included in the coconut fatigue. I could eat as much as I liked and satisfy my hunger. There were days when I even finished four coconuts a day. Some people said we might contract dysentery. We laughed at the idea.

The Japanese medical officer who inspected us frequently now became strict. We were given rest only when we had a temperature. The next day, we had to go to work. No quinine was given. Instead, a decoction of boiled papaya leaves or plantain tree pulp was administered. The Japanese said this was excellent medicine. Meena was helpless. He was obliged to carry out orders from above.

Although this particular barrack did not leak, the accommodation allotted to each man was less than three spans. We were in all 50 men. The congestion inside was too great. Added to the squalor and filthy smell as a result of dirty clothes and patients who never bathed, smoke was ordered to be diffused to kill malarial mosquitoes. Dirty, old, and torn mosquito nets, in which lice had made their homes, were given to us. On one occasion, the Japanese carried out mosquito net inspection. The portion immediately facing the Japanese was repaired, but the opposite side touching the side of the wall was not. The Japanese could sometimes be fooled easily.

April, May, and June 1945 dragged on wearily, wearing and tearing our bodies. The raiders were coming and going. They were preying on transport vehicles and huts. Each night, after going to bed, we would discuss the prospects of peace. The war was completing its sixth year, which was already too long. The Japanese had no supplies left. Their ammunition was becoming unusable. They, too, looked tired of the whole business. Our own condition was getting bad. If the war did not end by 1945, there was definitely no hope of our survival. It would have been better to have died earlier like the rest, but having undergone such a long ordeal, it would be most tragic to die now. No, no, we would see peace and better days. God would reward us. He had saved us from a thousand and one deaths. He would help us now, too. We were filled with fresh hope and a dogged determination to survive. It was a question of only a few months more. The war must be over by the end of 1945.

PEACE, RIOTING, & THE GOOD AUSTRALIANS

With these hopes and fears, we were passing our days. At the end of June, a Sikh NCO brought a cyclostyled leaflet dropped by an Australian aircraft. It was meant for the Kanakas and contained a few lines in the Kanaka language, which is a corruption of English. It went something like this:

New Guinea Boy:
The Tsere man I finish. Him and his soldiers I make prisoners. Now I plenty ship. Finishing Nippon. You now no helpm the fellow.

Our joy knew no bounds. Germany had been defeated. Thank God. Japan was now suing for peace, or would do so in three months' time at the latest. The brutes would not be able to stand the combined might of the Allies. The Australians did not effect a landing in New Britain for obvious reasons. Surrender would come from up above. It was all happening for our good. Our patience was being rewarded. Our men felt encouraged.

During these months, Rup Lal and Lance Naik Mohant Ram of 22 Battalion were of great help to me. Rup Lal and I ate together, and he shared with me whatever he could manage to get. Mohant Ram stitched our torn clothes and even washed them — something no one would have done in the circumstances. I did not belong to their unit, nor was of their place or caste. Yet they, realizing my helpless condition, did what they could to make me comfortable.

During my illness and anxiety, Rup Lal comforted me and was my constant companion. I can never forget these two gentlemen as long as I live, and pray to God that He may amply reward them.

Thefts of things in general and ration articles in particular were being severely punished by the Japanese. We heard that in the Hyderabad unit two men were beheaded for being in possession of half a sack of rice each. In our party, a sepoy (Mulla, we used to call him) stole a few seers of rice and was caught. He was given such a severe beating by Meena Gunsou [Staff Sergeant Meena] that a weaker man would have died.

Salt was more valuable than gold. For nearly a year, we did not have it. The man who arranged to possess a couple of seers was considered a wealthy man — on an equal status with the Ruler of a State. Everybody respected him and tried to befriend the lucky man. With a pinch of salt, even the few pieces of cold sweet potatoes that remained could be eaten, or a piece of raw papaya or coconut. Without salt, the situation looked gloomy. I would have parted with anything I possessed for few ounces of this precious stuff.

Our men succeeded in stealing a few seers from the Japanese. Their worry did not stop at this. Their greatest problem was how and where to hide it, for spies were alert watching our movements and would steal it. The owners filled the salt in bottles and buried them in pitch darkness. In spite of these secret maneuvers, one or two bottles were invariably found out and stolen. When the owner came to know of this, he would acquaint everybody present with the incident, warning the thief to replace them on pain of abuses and curses being showered on him. The thief did not mind these abuses. What he wanted was salt and he had got it, by fair or foul means. The owner would then shower a string of abuses on the thief, his father, sister, and when he came to the point of abusing the mother, the drone of a lone bomber — wou-wou-wou — would be heard. The other comrades would warn him of the approaching raider and entreat him to stop his abuses, as otherwise everybody might have to face death as a punishment for the sins of one man. And so, the man would be silent and begin his prayers. "Oh, Lord, save us from this impending calamity etc. etc. ..." The scene would be enacted the succeeding night all over again. And in this manner, the days passed.

The Japanese soldiers who took work from us were sometimes hinting to us about the war situation:

"Indo wakaruka? Ima na Itari Senzo Owari. Mussolini Na Number 10. Doitsu wa Ima Finish. Hitraru Kothai Toushou. Mo Sukoshi senzo owari . Indo Karg Naio. Mo Sukoshi Senzo Owari Indo Kang."

Meaning: *Do you know, Indians? Italy is defeated. Mussolini is a useless man. Germany is now finished. The assistants of Hitler are no good. In a short time, the war will be over and you will be able to return to India.*

These remarks, although uttered at random, meant much to us and confirmed our belief in the contents of the leaflet. The Japanese officers, having come to know of their subordinates' indiscretion, gave them a severe warning not to talk anything regarding war with Indians! After this an artificial silence was noticeable.

On 16 August 1945, an unusual panic pervaded the atmosphere. The Japanese were seen murmuring here and there, shouting nervously. Our two Japanese supervisors were also summoned to Battalion HQ. Something unusual had taken place. Had peace been declared? It would be too good to be true. Then why all this confusion? The next day, trench fatigue was not given. The men were asked to return without assigning any reason. We few were however busy with oil extraction.

One thing, however, was significant. There had been no bombing since 15 August 1945. On the 18th, a whisper went around that peace had been declared. This was casually announced by a Japanese nursing sepoy. But we could not believe it unless we heard officially. On the 19th as usual we were summoned for roll call. Meena Ginso appeared and with solemnity uttered these words:

"America Englishu Nippon Senzo Owari. Matta Indo Kaero. India Jothona."

Meaning: Peace Had Been Declared.[20]

That was the happiest day of my life. A second birth, resurrection from death, I thought. Now I would be returning to India, the India whose shores I left four- and -a -half years ago and to which I never hoped to return. I was free again after three-and-a-half years of captivity. I thanked God that he gave me that day. Everyone's face was now lit up with a bright smile. We went about joking, laughing, and singing, whereas our former captors cut a very sad figure. Our troubles had ended while theirs had just started. Meena — the good Meena,[21] our Japanese supervisor — said he would like to accompany us to India. He would not mind performing any type of job.

Most of us were in torn and tattered clothes, some with only a langoti, barefoot and bareheaded, with long beards, thin and emaciated bodies grown dark on account of three-and-a-half years' hard toil, wrinkled foreheads, and drooping eyes. With the majority of us, the hair had turned grey or fallen off due to increasing worry and care. This spectacle presented a striking contrast to that in which we first landed in Malaya: full of vigor, and fine specimens of manhood. Three and a half years of captivity under the Japanese had turned us into complete physical wrecks.

The next day we were supplied with the best of clothing available with the Japanese: shoes, hats, also plenty of quinine

---

[20] A more literal translation, I believe (or was told by a friend with some knowledge of Japanese), is the following: "America England and Japan have ended the war. You go back to India. India is a great country."

[21] My father named his only daughter Meena, and she turned out to be his most beloved child. Though, when I asked him the question in his old age, he could not remember, and though there is also a famous Indian movie actress of that period named Meena Kumari, I was to wonder if he did it in honor of the "good" Japanese soldier, Meena?

and other medicines. They told us the Emperor had commanded that all supplies and comforts be shared equally by the Japanese, Indians, and the Kanakas. The Japanese told us that Australians would be arriving soon and that until we were handed over to them, we would formally be under Japanese discipline. We didn't mind that.

Japanese soldiers were now seen busy dumping arms, transport vehicles moving to and fro with ammunition. We surmised the Japanese had surrendered unconditionally.

On 22 August 1945 we moved to Tabuna — 8 miles from D Lappan. A Japanese Lt. (Shukulta Chai) visited us and told us the Aussies might take a long time to arrive, and that we would have to obey the Japanese orders, to fatigue and economize. We had, however, heard that the Australians had already arrived in Rabaul and refused to do any type of fatigue. (Here I must give credit to the tactful leadership of a Havildar Kartar Singh.) Our men roamed about in the vicinity, pillaging Japanese gardens.

On 27 August, we were taken to Romali, about thirty miles from Rabaul, to be "handed over."

Romali turned into a collection point for all Indians in the vicinity. The Japanese left us there and departed — for good. Our three-and-a-half-year connection had finally ceased.

The Japanese who were in charge of our group HQ were stationed in Romali. Among others, they included Hiroshima Thai, Oobayashi Juni [Warrant Officer Oobayashi], Nakamura Socho [Sergeant Major Nakamura], Kabutha Chuui [First Lt. Kubota], et al. As an old revenge, Indians robbed their belongings and beat them up. The Japanese fled in fear of their lives, but as they had nothing to eat, they returned on the third day. They pleaded with the Indians to spare them, expressing profound regret for having ill-treated Indian prisoners. They were again beaten, but before they left, they were given food and assured that in future no harm would be done to them. The Japanese, having no clothes, bedding, or food, visited us again and again. Indians were by now moved to pity, and treated their former enemies with hospitality.

We were now quite comfortable. Our men went about ransacking Japanese dumps and bringing food stuffs such as fish, meat, sugar, and clothing. We gave them to the Kanakas in exchange for green vegetables.

Old feuds took the form of communal rioting in the camp. Mohammedans were the aggressors. Under the cover of darkness, they beat their Hindu or Sikh victims and called it "settling accounts." Mr. Ganapathi, a nursing Sepoy, was beaten, the charge against him being that he had carried tales to the Japanese about Indians.

The Dutch Malay soldiers had brought in a pig and killed it. Some Mohammedans battered a Malay to such an extent that he had to be carried to the hospital. The Malays expressed profound regret, saying they never knew it would offend Mohammedan religious sentiments and felt sorry that one of their comrades had been beaten mercilessly, even without a warning.

On another occasion a Sikh Havildar (Kartar Singh) was set upon by two Mohammedans (Alam and ?) who disappeared after beating him in the dark.

This enraged the other Sikhs who were on the spot. They abused the Mohammedans and challenged them to a straight fight. The former, although excelling in number, were unwilling to face the enraged Sikh Lions.

Indiscipline broke out. The senior, being only a Subedar of a Labor Corps, was not tactful enough to handle the situation.

In the middle of September 1945 a Prisoner of War Recovery Team had arrived from India. Major S.G. Rose was the Commandant. All RAPWI [Repatriated Allied Prisoners of War (Indian)] were ordered to concentrate at Karavi by the seaside (about thirty to forty miles from Rabaul) to await repatriation. We left for Karavi on 29 September 1945. There, too, no accommodation had been built; and so, "Build your own home as you go" proved too true till the end.

Mohammedans were accommodated in one camp, and Hindus, Sikhs, and others in another. It transpired that the Australians were quite willing to give as much comfort and rest to Indians as possible. But owing to the shortsightedness, I may even say meanness or racial prejudice of Major Rose, the offer of Japanese labor was turned down. Indians were ordered to build their own huts, without being provided any material. The Major feared "incidents" between Indians and the Japanese. The Chinese took advantage of this, and, with the help of the Japanese, had their huts constructed.

The Australians were prepared to gift 5 pounds (Rupees 55/-) to every Indian immediately. This offer was also refused by Major Rose.

As a result of this anti-Indian policy, our men were deprived of most of the concessions and amenities offered by the Australian staff.

The Australians were anxious to do as much for the Indians as possible. They gave us more than what we could eat, ungrudgingly, and better things than they gave their own soldiers — clothes, drinks, etc., etc. Australian soldiers would mingle freely and dine with us, disregarding all codes of etiquette. They hated the Americans and the British.

We love the Australians. They are simple.

John Baptist Crasta

WAR CRIMES AND THE RETURN HOME

At the end of September 1945, we were permitted to cable our next-of-kin in India. Airmail letters were also allowed.

On 1 October 1945, I was taken on the staff of the War Crimes Investigation Committee. Capt. McLillian and Capt. Foster of Auxiliary (India) Force, Capt. Munro, 1st Hyderabad Infantry, and I, comprised the staff. We were asked to investigate charges against the Japanese under the War Crimes Act, hold courts of Enquiries, collect evidence, et cetera and submit the proceedings to 11th Division HQ. This work kept me busy the whole day.

About one hundred and sixty proceedings were submitted, the most notable among them being a case of cannibalism. I give a precis. In April 1945, two men of the 13th Pioneer Company (Budhu Mistry, Giana Mistry) complained to the Japanese of illness, whereupon the men were given an injection. A couple of hours later, they died and were ordered to be buried. In the evening, a party of Indians was ordered to dig out the bodies. The Japanese cut out the arms and thigh muscles of the corpses, took out the livers, and placing these in four trays, carried them to their kitchen. The Indian batman was ordered to cook the flesh, which he refused, saying he would not cook human flesh. The Japanese thrashed the Indian for disobedience of orders and cooked the flesh themselves, after which, the officers, NCOs, and men sat down to a sumptuous meal.

A few days later, a Japanese was heard remarking to the senior VCO of the 13 platoon, that approval had been received from Tokyo for the killing and eating of Indians in New Britain. But the local HQ were not enforcing this, which fact had caused dissatisfaction among the Japanese ranks. [See the Notes at the end of this book for commentary on the subject of Japanese cannibalism during World War II.]

Another peculiar case which came to our notice was that of a Gurkha Viceroy's Commissioned Officer and an Other Rank. They were observed looking at a leaflet dropped by the Australian planes and were taken away by the Japanese Kempe Thai (Military Intelligence Police) on information given by a New Guinea Boy. The next day, they were seen hanging from a tree.

There were several other cases of beheading, shooting, and gross brutalities committed on prisoners. American and Australian airmen, on landing after being shot down, were immediately put to death.

The prisoners in New Guinea had fared a worse fate. Out of a total of three thousand men, only two hundred had survived. Most of them died of starvation, fatigue, and disease. Some had been eaten by the Japanese. In New Britain, out of a total of eleven thousand men, five thousand three hundred were alive, including nearly one thousand hospital cases.

The first batch of one thousand men left New Britain on 20 October 1945 by the aircraft carrier HMS "Formidable". The second batch left by HMS "Highland Chieftain" at the end of October, also Hospital Ship "Dorsetshire," which carried five hundred patients.

The third batch to leave on 14 November 1945 was ours — nearly a thousand men, on M.U. "Highland Brigade." Taking into consideration the situation then prevailing, arrangements on the ship were comfortable and satisfactory. The O.C. Troops, Lt. Col. Gregory, was very obliging, as were all the staff. I was accommodated in a second class dormitory reserved for Viceroy's Commissioned Officers.

Our accommodation, although congested compared to that when we left India, was sufficient, and the food was satisfactory. Cinema shows and entertainments by ENSA were regularly given. The other ranks also seemed to be satisfied.

On 19 November 1945, we passed by Morator, which presented a beautiful sight. On the 21st we halted for two hours at Kuching, Sarawak (British Borneo), and from our own ship's captain obtained directions regarding further movement.

I passed most of my time reading books and playing bridge with some army doctors. The voyage did me good. The rest, food, change of environment, and cheerful company improved my health. I was beginning to forget my previous life.

On the morning of 25 November 1945, the steamer touched Singapore harbor. ICOs and VCOs could go out into the city and return by midnight.

Three to four doctors and I left the ship after lunch and roamed about. Singapore was not even a tenth of what we had seen before.

Big shops had disappeared. There was no more of the gaiety and carefree life which had characterized Singapore. The small shops stocked a few things. "Capstans" cigarettes were sold at $ 4/- (Rupees 6/-) a packet, a cup of tea for 30 cents. Hotels were almost empty. We could not get a meal anywhere.

In the evening, we visited New World. My eyes could not believe it was the same place. New World, which was the center of attraction for people wishing to spend carefree evenings, was not entirely deserted. Those scenes of Chinese pageantry, plays, dance halls, and gambling, were now no more; but as if by habit, people flocked there still; and without remaining long, went away.

The Japanese in their greed had devastated every place which came into their possession, leaving poverty and misery as a legacy.

At Singapore, some RAF details and members of the ENSA joined us. We passed by Colombo on 2 December 1945 at noon and were disappointed to hear that the steamer would not make a halt there. Our voyage had already been long, and the ship's authorities decided we must reach Bombay as early as possible. So, speeding up, we reached Bombay on the morning of 4 December 1945.

We were having a glimpse of India after five years. Our happiness knew no bounds. The steamer berthed at No.2 Dock. Representatives of the Indian army, two Brigadiers and a Lt. Col. came aboard the ship and read out messages of appreciation and welcome from the King Emperor, the Viceroy and the Commander-in-Chief.

At 11 AM, we were entertained with refreshments by the Bombay Red Cross Committee. Sweets, cigarettes, and tea were served and a bag containing Red Cross gifts was presented to each of us.

We found Bombay and India in a much better condition than we feared we would.

In the evening, a "military special" train carried us to the Kalyan Rest Camp. This camp accommodated over 200,000 troops. Accommodation and food arrangements were satisfactory. We were told we would be dispatched to our respective depots as and when rail accommodation became available.

Days passed. Other units were being dispatched, but there was no news of when our turn would come. The camp authorities said they could not help it, as it all depended on priority arrangements. We were getting restless as we wanted to reach our homes as quickly as possible.

On 21 December 1945, at noon, we left for Ferozepore by a special train. The journey proved tedious as we got nothing to eat on the way. On the night of 24 December 1945, Christmas Eve, at 10 PM, we arrived in Ferozepore.

COMMENTARY AND BIOGRAPHICAL NOTES
BY RICHARD CRASTA

John Baptist Crasta

INVISIBLE BEGINNINGS: A SHORT EARLY HISTORY OF JOHN BAPTIST CRASTA

[Adapted from a Speech given by Richard Crasta, the minor co-author, editor, and publisher, on the occasion of the launch of the first edition of this book on December 30, 1997, simultaneously with his parents' 50th wedding anniversary.]

But we mustn't go too far back, must we, we mustn't go too far back in anybody's life. Particularly when they're poor. — Martin Amis, *London Fields.*

But I must, Martin, I must. I must go back to "the terrible smells, the terrible jolts" [Amis again], especially because my father was what some of his relatives might have called poor. And because he was my father, and because the story of his pain, his hard life, and his survival is all the more heroic to me precisely because of the terrible smells some writers would like to shrink from. And also because his old age prevents him from speaking for himself.

Besides, the account that follows is the gripping, sad, and yet life-affirming tale of a simple soldier caught in the middle of a war he did not choose to be in; besides which, it is somewhat short on biographical or atmospheric details which might enhance our understanding of its protagonist, his background, and his point of view. Let that be my opportunity, though I make no apologies for my utter subjectivity.

John Baptist Crasta (Prabhu was the ancestral family name, which he did not use in official records), whose son I claim to be in more ways than one, was born on 31 March 1910, in Kinnigoli, India — a remarkable achievement, because nothing has, does, or ever will happen in Kinnigoli. Luckily for it, the village has a road connecting it to the larger port-town of Mangalore, in the monsoon-drenched Southwestern pocket of India where little of earth-shaking importance has happened since the beginning of time, and where, during the first half of the 20th Century, tigers still roamed the surrounding villages and occasionally strayed into town, snacking on domestic animals and people, and biting off the fingers of a man preoccupied with answering the call of nature in the Great Outdoors at night.

My father was the firstborn of eight children, the others being Lucy, Antony, Aloysius or Louis, Ignatius, Bonaventure or Bonu, Margaret, and Gerald. Make that eight *thin* children. "We came from a family of thin people," said Uncle Louis, himself pretty thin despite ascending in mid-career to the world of medium-fat cats.

The Crasta children may have been thin in body, but their lives were thick with rosaries. "No rosary, no rice," was their Mater's domestic diktat: her homespun inversion of "No taxation without representation." Religious piety was a staple among these Konkani-speaking descendants of converted Catholics, refugees from the Portuguese Inquisition in late seventeenth century Goa, and survivors of Tipu Sultan's persecutions over a century later. And here, in a province long used to paternalistic British rule, in this verdant corner of a country where life was nasty, brutish, and often cut short by snake bites and other arbitrary interventions of nature, Catholic priests exercised awesome power over their flocks, threatening sinners and moral stutterers with hell and eternal damnation. "The priests were dictators!" declared the town's unofficial philosopher, raconteur, and freelance social analyst Dennis Britto.

My father's own father, Alex Dominic Crasta, was often absent from his life, working and living an inaccessible seventy miles from Kinnigoli in the mountainous jungles of the Western Ghats. "At one time, he owned four or five gadangs [toddy shops]," Uncle Louis remembers, adding the juicy detail that his father was a teetotaler. In my father's fuzzier memory, it is his mother who is awarded the credit for shaping his childhood. "My mother, my saviour," he characterized her recently in a quavering voice while gazing at her photograph, tears welling up his eyes.

Her name was Nathalia, and she was both a housewife and a provider. She would feed all her children first, and then eat the leftovers, if any (a not uncommon habit among Indian mothers; my mother, bless her, often did likewise, eating the chicken bones after all of us had wolfed down the lion's share of the meal she had lovingly and painstakingly prepared). One day, as she was massaging Baby Louis according to local custom, her two-year-old second son, Antony, had toddled off into an open well and drowned, despite her jumping in after him to save him. Later, still another son, Ignatius, succumbed to the bite of a rabid dog, there being no effective medicine for rabies at that time, at least none accessible to the indigent citizens of Kinnigoli.

"They took me away and didn't let me see the body," Uncle Bonu recalled later. "But I could hear them weeping loudly, inconsolably. Then they killed the dog."

"He was *sado* — simple and straight, never talked ill of anybody, never got into fights," my uncle Louis says of my father. When it came time to attend high school, my father walked the twenty miles to Mangalore, over hills, through roaring streams and patches of jungle, stopping at the "big houses" — meaning, the houses of the well-heeled — for a little free refueling, a glass of water and a piece of jaggery or large pieces of brown sugar, to revive his flagging energy. He found himself a room as a private boarder in Mangalore while attending Saint Aloysius College High School. One day, when his mother heard that he was sick, she, being too poor to afford the bus fare, carried Baby Gerald on her arm and walked the twenty miles to Mangalore to see him.

It is harder for a rich man to enter Heaven than for a camel to enter the eye of a needle (or for the rich man to enter the eye of a camel too, perhaps?), or so the Bible says; but it was always pretty easy for a rich man to enter St. Aloysius College and its high school, and to escape the whipping the padres gave to the fiscally and morally unlucky. After all, the college towered over property donated by the local squire, its chapel being a magnet, every Sunday, for the town's un-whipped cream of Catholic society. My father, though not one of India's wretched poor, was consigned by his family income to its struggling lower middle class. And often, because he had not paid his two-rupee monthly school fees on time, he was kicked out of his St. Aloysius High School classes by the Italian Jesuits who then ruled over this little scrap of the Indian empire, and who were the Official local representatives of Jesus Christ, Friend of the Poor.

Thanks to a last-minute loan, my father paid his examination fees and obtained his high school diploma. Mangalore still being a one-hundred-bullock-cart, fifteen-horse-carriage, seven-Model-T-Ford town with limited employment opportunities, most local high school graduates at that time had a habit of heading for the nearest metropolis, Bombay, to find a job. Thanks to the invitation of a family friend, Ignatius, my father hopped on to Karachi instead. Little did he know that he would go on to become a well-traveled man, though at least a quarter of that mileage was the result of the hospitality forced upon him by the Japanese.

After five years of assorted labor in Karachi, including, at one time, shoveling coals for a coal retailer, he joined the Army in 1933.

The next year, he learned of the death of his father. On Easter Sunday, 1934, my grandfather caught pneumonia, and it was decided to take him to the nearest hospital in Mangalore twenty miles away. The mode of transportation? The bullock cart of a friend. However, the cart's owner did the Christian or Mangalorean Catholic thing: he decided not to skip his Easter revels of booze and delicious pork and mutton curries eaten with soft rice cakes. Festive meals, which occurred about four or five times a year at Christmas, Easter, the parish feast, Our Lady's Nativity, and during wedding celebrations, were not to be sneezed at in those lean and hungry times. Thus, it was nightfall before the cart started for Mangalore with its human cargo, including one sozzled driver. When it reached Father Muller's Hospital the next morning, Dr. L.P. Fernandes, the head doctor, lifted the sheet, checked my grandfather's pulse, and said, "There's no point admitting him. He is dead." My grandfather's body, having joined The Dead shortly after the time that his friend had celebrated Jesus Christ's rising from it, was upgraded to taxi class on the return trip to his Kinnigoli graveyard.

The death was a blow to the family, especially because at the time, widows suffered many inconveniences and a steep fall in social status — though luckily, because my grandmother was a Christian, she was not compelled to shave her head. Also, in the absence of income, the coffee estate land that her husband Alex Dominic had been sanctioned reverted to the government for nonpayment of dues. My dutiful father, who had already been partly supporting the family, now lived even more frugally, sending all the savings he could spare to help support his mother and younger siblings.

And did this perfectly silly end to my grandfather's life make my father resolve that he would not easily become Death's victim? Possibly, for he narrowly escaped a devastating earthquake that struck Quetta the following year. And then, six years later, he found himself in a war, but survived, against all odds, to write the memoir that follows, keeping it safe for 51 years through dozens of army transfers until his son, by then a published author, discovered it and published it himself.

Perhaps it was not just God, but Life, too, which must have had a soft spot for my father, for he survived it all, including fifty years of a humble postwar existence in which his only vehicle was a bicycle fitted with a bell. Not only that, he saw many of his social, financial, and military superiors to their graves.

And now, ladies and gentlemen, I am proud to present to you my father, John Baptist Crasta, the author on a bicycle.

FATHERS AND SONS: A TALE OF LITERATURE, REINVENTION, AND REDEMPTION

In late 1997, nearly fifty-two years after he had written his memoir of being a POW of the Japanese during World War II, my father had nearly forgotten the manuscript's existence. "I don't know, I think it is lost," he stammered weakly when I asked him if he knew the whereabouts of the original. His wrinkled and sunbaked skin draped itself loosely around his frail bones, which he dragged about uncertainly in the small, dark rooms of the tiled mud structure he called home. In the previous three or four years, each time I visited him on my annual trips to India, I feared that it might be the last time I would see him. Now, he was sleeping at odd times in the day, rarely leaving home except to tip his hat to the Big One during the obligatory Sunday Mass. He walked slowly and hesitantly, first one short step, then another. He was not the defiantly active man I had known, the man with a contempt for death.

I had already left the icy winds of New York for the endless December sun of Southwestern India, secretly planning to surprise my father with an unusual fiftieth-wedding-anniversary gift: the first edition of his memoir and my humble wish that, just as his body had cheated death countless times in the eighty-seven years past, his spirit and his book would triumph over it for many more decades.

What made me do this, considering that at the time I had determined to publish it, I had still not read only a part of the manuscript — which I had quietly and protectively photocopied during my previous visit, a fact I wished to hide from him even at this late hour?

To answer this truthfully, I must take you back to my childhood, or perhaps to that universal state called childhood. I began by being proud of my father, as most children are in their age of innocence. But when I reached that awkward age when I was exposed to the materialistic judgements of the world, I was embarrassed that my father rode a bicycle rather than drove an old Austin like my uncle, that his shirt was tucked unevenly into his pants, that one leg of his trouser was cuffed higher than the other, that he looked like someone an upper class Mangalorean could dismiss and boss around. We had not learned to love our father simply for what he was — our father. Like many children, we played immature "My Daddy can whip your Daddy" games. And sometimes, to overcome our perceived disadvantage, I and my brother would reinvent our father, telling friends that he was an Army "Major" rather than the Subedar Major he really was — in other words, by giving him a significant promotion four levels above his real rank. But my father remained stubbornly himself, the man on a bicycle. He rode a bicycle in the sun and in the rain, in the day and at night, a "market bag" for fetching fish or vegetables usually suspended from its handlebar. Nothing could persuade him to abandon this humble vehicle, much scorned by Indians obsessed with middle class respectability, for a loftier mode of transportation: not the possibility that he might puncture the ballooning ego of his son, the Indian Administrative Service officer, not an improvement in his financial position late in life, and not even his children's offer to pay for his autorickshaw fare or to buy him a scooter after being provoked by the taunts of relatives. He rode his bicycle till he was seventy-six years old, whereupon he visited the

United States for four months to visit his expatriate son, and realized on returning that two culture-shocks — the first on reaching the United States and finding trees near JFK International Airport instead of the endless skyscrapers he had expected, and the second on returning to India after four months of two-wheeler deprivation — had rendered him incapable of resuming his bicycling career.

I mention these details simply to underscore the simplicity of the man, the humble position he occupied for most of his life, and the fact that life was not very kind to him except in granting him life and allowing him to cling on to it for almost as long as imaginable for a resident of a country where life doesn't count for much: given that its possession of the world's second largest population — or one-sixth of humankind — does not even entitle it to a permanent voice in the United Nations Security Council. The bicycle, at first an economic necessity, grew into a rusty, creaky, yet indestructible symbol of his contempt for the shallow status-consciousness of Mangalorean society, where upperclass persons living just next door to the church would drive to it rather than risk the shame of being spotted walking like the not-blue-blooded middle classes — who in turn would walk long distances rather than endure the shame of being spotted on bicycles, the conveyance of the decidedly lower middle classes or of the lower castes. We didn't understand, as children, that our father's old bicycle, the most visible symbol of his humble and self-effacing identification with India's poor, was a statement, a courageous statement, of scorn for the class system he otherwise accepted as inevitable.

Mangalorean upperclass society returned his contempt with compound interest. The callous Plymouths, Fiats, and Ambassadors of the rich drove dangerously close to him, often making him scamper off the road onto a stone-littered sidewalk to save himself. And yet, I mention the bicycle only as a symbol of his modest, unhonored life, a life in which he kept his story to himself. If it is true, as the nuns and priests assured me when I was a child, that God shows his special love for certain individuals by sending them gift parcels of suffering, then God loved my father a little more than He should have.

It saddened me, when I grew older, to think of his hardship-filled life, which makes mine seem like a bowl of aromatic, sweet payasam. Luckily, it was not just God, but Life, too, which must have had a soft spot for my father, for he survived it all, and saw many of his social, financial, and military superiors to their graves.

Consider the odds my father had overcome. What were the chances of an Indian born in 1910, when the Indian life expectancy was about 37, reaching the age of 88? About one in a thousand. In addition to which he narrowly escaped the 1935 earthquake that nearly wiped out Quetta in today's Pakistan, having left the city the previous night on an Army transfer order. Thereafter, he survived innumerable bombings and three and a half years as a prisoner-of-war of the Japanese.

After returning from the war in December 1945, grievously weakened and ill, my father was granted six months of sick leave, which he spent recuperating slowly in Kinnigoli, where he was gradually nursed back to health by his simple and overjoyed mother.

"He looked really sad and terrified," my uncle Louis remembers. "He was worried, in a bad mood. He would sleep a lot, and not talk to anyone." Uncle Louis didn't understand the reason: PTSD or posttraumatic stress disorder hadn't yet been invented, let alone become fashionable, and my father was reliving his wartime nightmares by writing about them; or perhaps he was simply exorcizing his ghosts by consigning them to paper.

He returned to his life under proud, demanding, and feudal Army officers in an independent India that had no soft spot for veterans of their former Masters' Army or its wars. He kept his memory of hell on earth bottled up for years and years, never revealing to us, his comics-reading, joke-loving children more than a few stray snippets about his wartime deprivations. And we, young and full of life, our heads full of the Beatles and of girls, didn't really listen, didn't really care. Indeed, we fell short in giving him even the respect that he was due as our father.

Forty-six years after he had penciled his war memoir on the yellowing stationery of the Mayor Footwear Co., Kinnigoli, his brothers' footwear store in Kinnigoli, my first novel was published in India, and despite its prohibitive price (the hardcover was priced at half the monthly salary he had retired on), he went unprompted to a bookstore and bought it with his own money, and read it within two days.

This brought me closer to him, as did his age, and his growing weakness, which made me feel protective towards him. Still another was my experience of paternal love for my own children, and an understanding of how special it is to be a father. I have three sons; the sons are the fathers of the man.

Also, as I began to battle with my own too-obvious human limitations, my eyes were opened to his own special qualities — his stoicism, his simplicity, his hard work, his sense of humor, his disdain for superficial appearances and other people's opinions, his need to do the right thing, his insistence on continuing to work for more than thirty years after his official retirement from the Army, tottering precariously to his office right until the time he was nearly 87. I saw now that the man on the bicycle was having the last laugh at status-conscious Mangalore. His bicycle had kept him healthy, at least until the time that bicycling in increasingly polluted and traffic-choked Mangalore became more hazardous than beneficial to one's health.

Belatedly, I tried to honor him, dedicating my books to him: first, the British paperback edition of *The Revised Kama Sutra*, followed by my second book, *Beauty Queens, Children, and The Death of Sex*. In the meantime, I was also sending him money to help improve his extremely modest life style. But I still felt irreparably in his debt.

And when I first offered, in 1996, to publish his memoir, he declined. It was simply his modesty and his diffidence as to whether the story would interest anyone at all. He was also concerned that he might cause offence; perhaps the story should not be resurrected from its paper graveyard? I was disappointed, aware of my still-unpaid debt of love and honor. For I hadn't really submitted to him with unconditional and clearly expressed love until his memory and mental alertness, which hadn't deserted him until the age of 85, began to decline. He did not wish to travel any more, and my long-cherished fantasy of our meeting in the holiday atmosphere of a cool hill station, of having long and profound conversations leading to a deeper understanding and meeting of minds and hearts — a timeless father-son bond — could never be fulfilled. I realized I would have to take the initiative. I decided to "make" him an author (to the extent that we can "make" anyone what they are not), even if it meant going against his recently expressed intention. I decided, in other words, to reinvent my father — and on the grand battlefield of life to help him outrank his fellow Subedar Majors and perhaps some significantly higher brass.

I had a secret reason for doing so. Once, in my teenage years, when I had already sold my first few articles to a newspaper and begun to think of myself as a writer, I had come across the manuscript, judged its simple and straightforward style as falling below "literary" standards, and attempted to destroy it. Miraculously, it had survived, but the memory of my arrogance had remained within me like a guilty secret, making me even guiltier when a few years back I heard that the unremarkable and nearly unreadable memoirs of a Kansas grandmother had fetched a million-dollar advance from an American publisher.

I secretly started the publication process in early December 1997, tactfully extracting his conditional assent: "If we find the manuscript, it will be okay to publish it." Not the fullest permission, I grant, but when I regarded his entire life in context, and distilled from it its meaning and his true intention, I felt that he really wanted the memoir to be published. Because one writes to be read, even if one sometimes denies it to oneself.

Besides, he made me. Whatever I am, I would not be today but for his escape from being eaten by the Japanese or otherwise killed in the war, and for his marriage to my mother, Christine. So I owe my very existence to the story detailed in this book. It is therefore my story as much as his.

Furthermore, but for my risky decision, it is quite possible that this story would have been lost to history. As a writer, I believe so strongly that something is preferable to nothing, and that in conjunction with our art, our stories are our planet's most precious — and once written down, immortal — heritage, that I decided to take the risk of assuming his full permission. He would then have the option of blaming me if the book didn't get a good reception, and of accepting the credit if it turned out fine.

Besides, his original refusal came from some ancient sense of gentlemanliness and decency, some archaic sense of goodness. But, as Mae West said about her career and life, and as I say about publishing, goodness has nothing to do with it. Publishing is about initiative, about taking risks, about a passion for telling the truth.

Most of the time, history is written by the victors. Sometimes, it is also written by the powerful members of the vanquished side. I would help my father's voice become part of its truth. For I now believed that history should never be whitewashed; or else, if as some say we are condemned to repeat it anyway, how much the worse it would be to repeat it without even knowing that we were doing so. Only after the historical truth has been recorded, in this view, is forgiveness or realistic acceptance a soul-cleansing possibility for all concerned; for how can we forgive an act whose existence we are unaware of?

So I plunged into the secret production of *Eaten by the Japanese*. The day before my parents' fiftieth anniversary celebration, I caught the airplane from sunny and cool Bangalore on the Deccan Plateau to steamy, coastal Mangalore, and presented myself a few hours later at the park-like home of my friend, Dr. Kumar Arunachalam, a Mangalore author, polymath, and nature lover. Presenting him with the first edition just hot off the press, I requested him to read it the same day. If he liked the book, would he speak briefly at the celebration mentioning his appreciation of the book? And if he didn't like it, would he kindly keep his opinions to himself and decline the offer to speak — in deference to my father's age and his understandable state of shock when he discovered that he had become an author?

Dr. Arunachalam not only turned up the next day at the church hall, he spoke with such emotion that he couldn't be stopped even by noisy and fidgety children. He ended his long and passionate speech by calling my parents his own parents (even though he had never met them before that day), and by touching their feet before one hundred and twenty people in a surprising and dramatic gesture of respect and reverence. Dr. Arunachalam, who as a renowned local speaker and Vice-Principal and Dean of the local medical college wields considerable clout, explained later that the gesture had been spontaneous, and that a spontaneous gesture of touching someone's feet — contrasted with the ritualistic gesture, made at a wedding towards your parents or older relatives — is an expression of total submission and a declaration of insignificance before the greatness of the person whose feet were being touched.

The man on the bicycle had come a long way. Tears misted my eyes.

The event ended in smiles. Until the final moment, I had feared an explosion from my father and even a public scene: "How dare you do this without my permission? I disown the book!" Instead, he looked around mystified for a few minutes, and then smiled. Fifteen minutes later, I observed him autographing books as if he had been doing it all his life.

It was one of the happiest moments of my life.

But I considered that moment to be a pure gift, a bonus I didn't necessarily deserve. Because by then, I had accepted him completely, as well as the lesson he had taught me: that to have suffered through a rough life, and to have smiled and survived, is to have been a hero.

* * *

Despite the book's launch before a large Mangalorean audience, and passionately commendatory reviews in local papers by Dr. Kumar Arunachalam and by local literary personality Louella Lobo Prabhu, the hurriedly produced book had been marred by printer's devils, inhibiting its presentation to a more sophisticated national audience. I decided to bring the book out properly before a larger audience, persuading myself that my literary career could not proceed unless I first did justice to my father.

But there was another, non-literary duty to be performed before I could feel some degree of liberation from that powerful sense of incompleteness in my relationship with my father. Dr. Arunachalam's gesture of touching my father's feet, repeated later by another Mangalorean I greatly respect, Konkani musician, composer, and impresario Eric Ozario, had haunted me. Because, having been an individualistic, city-raised Christian too cut off from my culture and even from my Indian Christian village roots, I had never touched my father's feet. Back in America, I feared that I would never forgive myself if my father passed away from this world without my ever having touched his feet, while others — no doubt my brothers, kindred souls, and cosmic, Brahmanic extensions of myself — had done so.

In October 1998, ten months later, I arrived in a monsoon-lashed Mangalore and dashed home from the airport, heading directly for my father's bedroom. He didn't come out to greet me as he usually did, for he was weaker than before, slowly losing his once-solid grip on the world. I walked right in and hugged his frail frame, paused a few seconds, and then bent my once-proud body and touched his feet.

He died in October 1999, exactly one year later, with me being present at his hospital bedside — and I consider myself extremely fortunate and blessed to have done all that I did before he passed away.

KILLING TO EAT

Claudius: Where's Polonius?

Hamlet: At supper, my Lord. Not where he eats, but where he is eaten.

— Hamlet, William Shakespeare

Like my father, I grew up imbibing "Christian" precepts such as: *Forgive those that trespass against us. Love your enemy. Turn the other cheek.* So why have I chosen for my father's war memoir a title reflecting a terrible moment in Japanese history rather than the extremely polite, peace-loving, and orderly people who now inhabit the country of Japan? Is not Japan, the only country to have two atomic bombs tested on its people, a much-beaten nation deserving of delicate handling?

This thought, and my passionate love for Japanese cuisine (unrelated to some of the grislier portions of this book), along with a respect for Japanese culture which may have started with my donning a kimono for a minor female part in Gilbert and Sullivan's *The Mikado*, in which I even sang a song in butchered Japanese ("Miya sama, miya sama . . . "), delayed the second edition of this book for awhile.

Also, just before this book went to press, when the past and the present had begun to loosen their grip on my father — it being a struggle for him to name the country that had dropped the atomic bomb, or the island where he had been held captive — he had yielded up a touching story.

When the second atomic bomb vaporized the heart of Nagasaki, and the order came from the Japanese High Command to my father's captors to lay down arms and free their prisoners, my father's Indian colleagues, being suddenly on the victorious side, wished to exact revenge upon their former captors and tormentors. And my father tried to stop them with the words, "Now that we have the power, we should treat them well." It was not just his charitable spirit triumphing over the hatred in his heart, but his respect for the rule of the law. However wrong his former captors, he believed, they deserved justice under the process of the law.

This spirit of magnanimity being of a piece with the memoir itself, it was only after much reflection and debate that I decided to stick to my original inspiration for the title, *Eaten by the Japanese.*

That original inspiration had resulted from a son's anguish at reading his father's memoir. It was strengthened by my sorrow at Japan's continuing refusal to apologize or make reparations for its use of "comfort women," the rape of Nanking, and other war crimes (Iris Chang, author of The Rape of Nanking, whose book I had the ghastly misfortune to look through during this period, was quoted in a newspaper as saying that this refusal of the Japanese constitutes the second rape of Nanking). And it was rounded off by the thought that even if my father in his most charitable moments wished to put his past behind him, was it necessary or right that his nightmare be hidden from history? That was unthinkable, because the story was now at least somewhat bigger than my father, having begun to encompass his son's quest for justice — on his father's behalf—at least to the extent that the story be told and heard around the world. And his son's belief that justice is sometimes achieved by assertiveness and passion — the squeaky wheel syndrome, which applies to the titles of books as much as to their contents — rather than by bashfulness and disengagement, and that the writing of history, even personal history (for all history is ultimately personal), is a sacred act that must not make compromises with the truth.

My father was traumatized, humiliated, starved, and deprived of his freedom for three-and-a-half years, cut off from contact with his family and mother, not knowing if she was alive, while she in turn did not know if he was. He never forgot that during his absence, she refused to attend any form of merriment, any wedding or celebration, mourning him as if he were her third son to be claimed by Death. While he was a prisoner of the Japanese, and during the long wait to be shipped home and the months that he spent in recovering his bodily strength and his emotional equilibrium from 3.5 nightmare years, his colleagues in India were quickly promoted to fill the newly created vacancies, and he never caught up. While Britain and Japan rose from the ashes of 1945 to become two of the richest nations on earth, my father lived the next five decades of his life struggling to feed and educate his family, and died in very humble circumstances.

But there was also another current and continuing injustice, which resonated with the darker passages in my father's memoir. I remembered a poignant remark by my fellow-Indian writer, Pico Iyer. He had said, in an interview, that being married to a Japanese woman and living in Japan was a difficult fate for him, because in Japan today, "Indians are the lowest of the low." In other words, to the Japanese (and no doubt this is an imperfect generalization), many of whom revere the Buddha that India gave to the world, we Indians are so low-down in the food chain, so picayune that it does not appear to matter, to them or to the world, that thousands of us were mistreated, tortured, killed, enslaved, and eaten during World War II. It simply is not a part of their consciousness, and while they greatly respect Americans today, bending over backwards — but mostly forwards — to imitate their culture and impress them, they are often dismissive of India. In fact, about a year ago, Japan felt morally superior enough to be one of the first countries to cut off economic aid to India after its May 1998 nuclear explosions.

"Most of all, I think it is important that this book should be read, especially by the Japanese," said my American friends

Dave and Faye Cohen, arguing for the title's power to attract attention, and contributing a Jewish perspective: that of remembrance and the power of speaking out. "The Japanese who think themselves so superior should be able to face the fact that they descended to such savagery."

And though I believe all of us have within us a dark side, and that in a profound sense we are also the Other, it is also important, in the illusory everyday world that we call Reality, that we append the stories of the weak and the voiceless to the histories written by the mighty and the once-mighty, and that each us of register our horror, our personal footnote, to the Official and often Sanitized Communal History. Any lingering doubts I may have had about the title disappeared after I met Roger Mansell, an American war historian who had been examining the Japanese record in World War II. Mansell was horrified by the lack of remorse in a recent Japanese compendium of World War II recollections called Senso. He explained that American G.I.s had been cannibalized simply as an act of demoralization; these acts had nothing to do with the nutritional needs of the Japanese. So I decided to retain the title for this second, public edition, even allowing in a moment of optimism that the book might receive attention in Japan and persuade the Japanese to confront and admit to their widely observed racism and start a national campaign to tackle it, making it less possible for a future Pico Iyer to say, "In Japan, an Indian is the lowest of the low."

Besides, why should it be so hard for the Japanese to issue an apology to all the Indians who were so abused and manipulated, and to their children and descendants? Will not that hasten the process of healing and forgiveness?

It is a consummation devoutly to be wished. Or at least to be dreamed. For only the truth will set us free, and set free the souls of our deceased brothers and sisters, and above all, the souls of the Japanese themselves and of their ancestors.

NOTES

The Indian National Army: Brigadier Ferris and Colonel Cyrus Dalal, both retired Army officers from Bangalore, rendered valuable assistance with the names of military units and the history of the Indian National Army. As I heard it from them: after the war, the British regime tried three of the Indian National Army fighters for treason on the charge of "waging war against the King." But the trial was controversial, given understandable Indian nationalist support for those who had risked their lives for India's freedom, and the men were acquitted. Once India attained independence, Prime Minister Nehru tried to get the Indian Army to absorb the former Indian National Army volunteers. However General Cariappa, the Army's Commander-in-Chief, is supposed to have told him (in the Brigadier's words): "Can't do it. It will be the end of the army in India." The reason? The soldiers who had remained loyal to the British, and who formed the vast majority of the Indian army, considered the INA men to be violators of their supreme oath of loyalty to their officers, and therefore as turncoats or JIFS (Japanese Inspired Fifth Columnists). The induction of the latter into the regular army might lower the morale of the others: so felt the General and the senior army commanders. Nehru accepted General Cariappa's recommendation, and the former INA soldiers were discharged.

My father's claim, in his memoir, that INA men had engaged in the torture of Indians who refused to join the Japanese side, was confirmed by Colonel Cyrus Dalal, who said his uncle had himself been a victim (when contacted, the uncle declined to comment, explaining that he was busy writing his own book). Brigadier Ferris added that the Japanese themselves had a poor opinion of the INA fighters, especially after a group of them, in Northern Burma, surrendered to the British without a fight, giving up a cache of precious arms and ammunition. "Following that, the INA recruits were supplied with brooms by the Japanese, who claimed the Indians were only fit to be sweepers." This observation, though possibly controversial and representing Japanese racial prejudice, needs to be mentioned if for no other reason but a writer's duty to truthfully report what he heard.

Brigadier Ferris was one of the first Indians to be commissioned into the British Indian Army, in which, before that time, British commissioned officers had commanded "native" soldiers. "By and large they were fair and square," he said of the British, his colleagues. However, they did have some prejudices, he admitted. "Indians can't fly multi-engine aircraft," the British said. Less than forty years later, these Indians or their descendants had managed a sizeable air force and squadrons of jet fighters in three wars, and had exploded an atomic device.

Cannibalism by Japanese Soldiers during World War II: Among other references to cannibalism is an e-mail from Roger Mansell, a reviewer of military books, to the distinguished Brooklyn poet and publisher Harry Smith, saying that cannibalism was practiced upon American GIs during the battle for the liberation of Luzon, Saipan, and Okinawa. He says, "It was not about starving, but a way to totally demean the enemy, to wit, the Americans." During the subsequent war crimes trials, some Japanese soldiers were convicted of having participated in the cannibalism of American military personnel.

From Wikipedia, I quote:

In some cases, flesh was cut from living people: another Indian POW, Lance Naik Hatam Ali (later a citizen of Pakistan), testified that in New Guinea:

"The Japanese started selecting prisoners and every day one prisoner was taken out and killed and eaten by the soldiers. I personally saw this happen and about 100 prisoners were eaten at this place by the Japanese. The remainder of us were taken to another spot 50 miles [80 km] away where 10 prisoners died of sickness. At this place, the Japanese again started selecting prisoners to eat. Those selected were taken to a hut where their flesh was cut from their bodies while they were alive and they were thrown into a ditch where they later died."

Editorial Notes and Changes: Editorial remarks have been made in square brackets [like this], in footnotes, and in these notes. Any remarks within parentheses (like this) are the author's own. An attempt was made to be faithful to the obviously unedited original, and not to substitute the genuineness of the author's voice and idiom with politically correct terms or with the Queens' English, except in a few places where "Japs" has been changed to "Japanese" (this has been done in most such cases to soften the tone, but has occasionally *not* been done so that the historical authenticity of the record, and of his voice, can be reproduced as closely as possible); there has also been some very minor editing in places where an exact reproduction of the original manuscript might have rendered the book confusing or incomprehensible to the reader. The chapter divisions and chapter headings are those of the editor, and were devised to make the narrative more accessible and digestible; the original was an unbroken and untitled, handwritten memoir: written, amazingly, with a lead pencil.

John Baptist Crasta

KEY DATES IN JOHN BAPTIST CRASTA'S LIFE

1910: Born in Kinnigoli, Mangalore.

1933: Joins the British Indian Army at the age of 23.

1942: 15 February: the British surrender Singapore, and John Baptist Crasta becomes a Prisoner of War of the Japanese.

1945: 19 August, is officially informed by the Japanese that the war is over.

1945: December 4, sets foot in India for the first time in five years.

1947: At 37, he is married to 19-year-old Christine, a fellow Konkani Mangalorean Catholic, on December 27.

1948: Tour of duty in the India Pakistan war over Kashmir.

1949: His first child, Franklin, is born.

1958: His fourth and last child (and only daughter), Meena, is born when he is 48 years old; she would always be his favorite child.

1965: Retires from the Army at age 55, the official retirement age at the time. Returns to Mangalore.

1986: Visits the United States to see his son, Richard, and his family, and briefly makes a trip to Canada to visit a friend, Ignatius — this is his first foreign trip after his return from captivity forty years earlier, in 1946. It is also his last.

1997: *Eaten by the Japanese*, the first edition, is published, and presented to him during his 50th wedding anniversary celebration.

1999: Dies in October, at the age of 89, after falling and breaking his hip.

2000: *Eaten by the Japanese*, the second edition is officially published with a quiet book launch in New Delhi. The launch is attended by Dhirendra Singh, Additional Defence Secretary, who would soon become the Principal Home Secretary of India. In 2001, Richard Crasta is invited to meet the Indian Army Chief of Staff, General V.P. Malik, and formally present him a copy of the book, and does so at Army Headquarters, New Delhi.

ABOUT THE AUTHORS

John Baptist Crasta was born in 1910 in the village of Kinnigoli, near the town of Mangalore in Southwestern India. He joined the British Indian Army (later the Indian Army) in 1933, serving in Quetta, Karachi, Singapore, New Britain (involuntarily), Bangalore, Jammu & Kashmir (war service), Bombay, Panagar, Calcutta, and Bareilly, and winning the Indian Independence Medal, the 1939-1945 War Service Medal, The George VI 1939-1945 Star, the George VI Pacific Star, and the Jammu & Kashmir Medal. He was appointed as a Viceroy's Commissioned Officer in 1946, and a Junior Commissioned Officer in 1948. He married Christine in 1947, and together they had three sons and one daughter.

Eaten by the Japanese was first published with a publication date of 1998 by his son, Richard Crasta, who was by then an internationally published author. The memoir was formally presented to the public and also to his surprised father as an act of gratitude on the occasion of the latter's 50th wedding anniversary on December 27, 1997. Until his death in October 1999 at the age of 89, John Baptist Crasta lived a simple life in a quiet Mangalore locality, and bicycled to work every day until he was 75. He may be the oldest first-time Indian author ever, and this is his only book.

His son **Richard Crasta**, the publisher, editor, and minor co-author of this book, is the author of seven other books including *The Revised Kama Sutra: A Novel,* which has been published in ten different countries and in seven languages. He has also published a number of e-books on major e-book platforms. For information, please visit richardcrasta.com

CPSIA information can be obtained at www.ICGtesting.com
Printed in the USA
LVOW10s0706180214

374150LV00029B/493/P

9 781480 034051